SPIRIT AND TRADITION:
AN ESSAY ON CHANGE

Spirit and Tradition: An Essay on Change

by

STEPHEN PLATTEN

and

GEORGE PATTISON

The Canterbury Press
Norwich

© Stephen Platten and George Pattison 1996

First Published 1996 by The Canterbury Press Norwich
(a publishing imprint of Hymns Ancient & Modern Limited,
a registered charity)
St Mary's Works, St Mary's Plain,
Norwich, Norfolk, NR3 3BH

British Library Cataloguing in Publication Data

A catalogue record for this book is available
from the British Library

ISBN 1-85311-130-9

*Typeset by David Gregson Associates, Beccles, Suffolk
Printed and bound in Great Britain by
Antony Rowe Ltd, Chippenham, Wiltshire*

TO

To the churches of Badwell Ash, Great Ashfield, Hunston, Langham and Stow Langtoft in the Diocese of St Edmundsbury and Ipswich and the church of St Peter, Vauxhall, in the Diocese of Southwark.

CONTENTS

ACKNOWLEDGEMENTS

The authors and publisher gratefully
acknowledge the kind permission of
the following sources to quote from:
How Far Can You Go? by David Lodge
(p. 89) Penguin Books/Reed Consumer Books;
Place of the Lion by Charles Williams
(pp. 14–15, 40–41, 43, 151 and 203–4)
Wm B. Eerdmans Publishing Co, USA/
Faber & Faber UK; *Tradition and Traditions*
by Yves Congar (pp. 263, 264–5, 268–9)
Search Press Ltd/Burns & Oats Ltd.

Introduction

The arrival of a new incumbent in a parish within the Church of England is often approached by many with some apprehension. Will he be another one of those 'new brooms' ready to sweep clean all the cherished traditions which have characterised the life of this parish over the years? Others have precisely the opposite fear. Will it be more of the same? Shall we never receive anyone with the vision to break out of the mould which has fossilised our corporate life for so long? Undoubtedly this experience could be related too by Roman Catholics welcoming a new priest or by Free Church people looking to the arrival of a new minister. Part of what lies behind such hopes, fears and apprehensions is a variety of different perceptions of what we might mean in the Christian Church by tradition.

It is often remarked that if a particular ritual is repeated more than once in the public domain then it constitutes a tradition. We have the prayers of intercession from the back of the Church in St Saviours – its always been our tradition. In fact it probably started with the previous vicar. In this case tradition is undoubtedly seen as something which inhibits change. It stands for the status quo, whether viewed positively or negatively.

Another word which is equally commonly bandied about on the occasions of the arrival of a new priest or minister is the word 'Spirit'. This is perhaps endowed with a still greater diversity of 'hinterland' in its nuances and meanings. If someone is 'filled with the Spirit' he may be a charismatic, or he may simply be someone who is seen as displaying a manifest holiness. If a person is described as having 'a tremendous Spirit' then it may be interpreted still more widely; it may not even have a directly religious connotation. Whatever is meant in each particular case, Spirit is often equated with liveliness and also quite frequently with change.

Linked with these often stereotyped reactions is an unhelpful polarization that reaches down into Christian theology and life far more deeply than simply at the level of the personality and gifts of individual ministers of the gospel. Radical and conservative, modernist and reactionary, tradition and Spirit are pairs of terms which we often see juxtaposed. In making judgments based on such contrasts, much often centres on attitudes to worship and whether the services in a particular church will remain the same.

One of the reasons why liturgical change is invariably the focus of such intense debate is that it is (rightly) intuited as involving a much wider re-evaluation of the Church's life and self-understanding. The context for such change is thus not only social (the needs of a changing society) but also theological, that is, to do with how the Church thinks and feels about itself, that is, its self-understanding. It is our intention here to step back from the immediate interface between Church and society as that is experienced in local Church communities in order to look more at the theological context of liturgy, and the life of the Church. We shall focus on such fundamental theological resources as doctrine, scripture, Spirit and tradition. These are shown to exemplify the inner impetus of the Church towards change and development. The processes at work in this impetus are then shown in connection with such themes as ecumenism, images and archetypes, art, architecture and music, before finally an attempt is made to show how they may also be discerned in forms of life outside the Church.

We have deliberately been eclectic in gathering together the material which we hope demonstrates our understanding of Spirit and tradition. The sort of stereotyped responses which we have set out above all too easily confine and restrict reflection on change within the Christian Church. So, for example, even our attitudes to ecumenism can be surprisingly predictable. Indeed when people are attempting to label members of various traditions they may even mark them off as conservative, liberal, high church, low church or 'ecumenical'. The ecumenical movement itself can easily fall into the danger of producing a static self-identity which marks it off from the rest of the life of the separate churches.

Then there is the realm of images. People often like to tell us that we no longer live in a world where images matter. It is hard to understand how that argument could stand when one looks at the dominant role of the media in forming opinion and in communicating in our contemporary world. Some advertisers only need to place their trademark on the television screen – no words are necessary. Christianity has depended throughout its history on certain controlling images, but it has also always been prepared to use images contemporary to a particular society to convey the meaning of the gospel. The myths of a particular age are not the equivalent of fairy stories but rather the controlling images and models which help us to understand and to communicate with each other within a particular society. How can those of us who contribute to the life of the Christian community better understand the part that such images and archetypes play?

Reflection upon the importance of imagery takes us almost directly into the arts. Over the centuries, so much western art has been dominated by images from the Christian tradition and indeed has been produced through the patronage of the Christian Church. How do such images convey the developing tradition of the Christian gospel and how are they themselves changed in the process? Similar questions can be asked about music; in both music and the visual arts we have passed through a time of critical questioning where some have seen a complete break in tradition with the advent of modernism. Such reflections come together when we begin to look at the nature of the building in which we worship and in which our liturgies are performed. How do images and artistic tradition find themselves in a dialectical relationship with theology such that they help to form our own experience within Christian worship?

Finally, and already hinted at, is the crucial question of how Christianity relates with culture in general. Different theologians have started from different standpoints. Paul Tillich began with culture and moved to the gospel. Karl Barth, it is argued, began with the gospel and moved out into culture. Except in very particular circumstances and communities (presumably monastic orders might be one example and even there the relationship is complex) the Christian Church has never and indeed could never exist isolated from the culture within which it is set. Nevertheless that does not deny the fact that the particular relationship between culture and theology, gospel and the world, can vary greatly. It is a debate which is not exclusive to Christianity amongst the great world religions. It is an essential part of our reflection upon what we might mean by Spirit and tradition and of our understanding of the nature of change within the Christian Church.

Our discussion within this book, then, is consciously removed from the immediacy of the sort of debates about change likely to be met directly in parish life. We hope that by doing this we may provoke a greater awareness of presuppositions regularly made in reflecting upon practical matters of liturgy, evangelism and Christian living. Especially we regard it as good news for local church communities in their concern to find an appropriate way of witnessing in and to the contemporary world, since it breaks the deadlock between conservatives and innovators by showing that the very tradition of the church is what it is precisely by virtue of its dynamic and innovative character. Our vision might not inappropriately be described as radically conservative, since it involves a positive appraisal both of the traditional resources of the church and of the spirit of change at large in contemporary church life.

Michaelmas 1995   GEORGE PATTISON
                                                    STEPHEN PLATTEN

Chapter 1

Christian Belief – Continuity or Controlled Change?

'The Times They Are A'Changin''

> Austin Brierly almost rubbed his eyes in disbelief sometimes. He read the professional theological journals with much the same mixed feelings of shock and liberation as Michael read *Lady Chatterley's Lover* and the sexually explicit fiction that was published in its wake. Of course the theologians and exegetists were generally more discreet than the novelists. They expressed themselves with elaborate caution in learned journals of tiny circulation, or exchanged ideas with like-minded scholars in private. It was understood that one did not flaunt the new ideas before the clergy, most of whom were deplorably ill-educated and still virtually fundamentalists when it came to the interpretation of the New Testament.[1]

Ignoring the dismissal of all clergy as intellectually bankrupt and ill-read, these comments, the reflections of a novelist, characterise a common perception of the Second Vatican Council of 1962–1965. Although the Council could legislate only for the Roman Catholic Church, nevertheless it was part of a wider ferment and renewal of the Christian Churches manifested in a variety of different and sometimes terrifyingly radical ways during the 1960s and since. Given its influence and the wider movement of which it was part, reflection upon the Council and the historical developments of which it was in some sense the culmination remain of significance to the Christian churches more widely.

Convened by Pope John XXIII and sustained by Pope Paul VI, Vatican II was undoubtedly the single most significant event amongst these movements in the Christian Church this century. Indeed it is now almost commonplace to note that some of the changes that the Anglican and Reformed

Churches have taken four hundred years to digest and consolidate happened to the Roman Catholic Church within the space of ten years. David Lodge's novel from which the opening extract is taken parodies the period of the Council and examines some of its effects. The shift described in the novel, is one where inquisition is exchanged for the libertine, legalism for antinomianism, authoritarianism for permissiveness. In the world of theology it has wrought momentous changes still being fought over in the dialogue between Cardinal Joseph Ratzinger and Professors Edward Schillebeeckx, Hans Küng, and a whole host of other Catholic theologians. Indeed it is a debate not restricted to Catholics; Anglicans, Lutherans and Reformed have equally keenly debated the nature of the Church and the nature of Christian dogma and moral teaching, and particularly in the period since 1960.

David Lodge makes no secret of the perceived link between the theology of the Council and such contemporary *causes célèbres* as the *Lady Chatterley* trial. At the theological level one might also draw attention to the debate surrounding Bishop John Robinson's *Honest to God*, the internal and external pressures of political radicalism within the Churches (particularly heightened by the Vietnam War), and the acceleration of liturgical change in the Church of England, with the onset of the era of 'Series 1, 2 and 3' and 'worship by booklet' rather than in a solid hardback volume. In this way, Vatican II can easily be seen as symbolic of a wider sense of crisis throughout the Christian West that emerged into the public realm in the 1960s and has gathered momentum ever since. On this same trajectory we might also locate more recent controversies such as those provoked by liberation theology (in the Roman Catholic Church) and by the ordination of women and the radical theology of the 'Sea of Faith' movement (in the Church of England).

Vatican II – Newman's Council

The psychological effect of Vatican II was enormous and understandably led to something of a theological identity crisis over the nature of tradition. In the 1970s a cynical commentator noted: 'A Catholic theologian spends many years discovering a new insight and then just as many years proving that it is not really new.'[2] This reflection is less true now than it was in the past and, despite continuing controversy and debate, other indicators point to the permanent change that has taken place. So, for example, academic books containing the *imprimatur* and *Nihil obstat* are now in the minority. Theologians offer their work within the atmosphere of open international scholarship, even if on some occasions it has meant the loss of their licence or teaching accreditation by the Church. Despite an unease that there are now many within the Roman Catholic Church who regret the effects of Vatican II, the new world which it heralded not only for Roman Catholics but for all the Churches is here to stay.

Many theologians have described Vatican II as 'Newman's Council' in the sense that the Council and the new world it presaged consciously promulgated the teaching of John Henry Newman albeit more than seventy years after his death. It should not be assumed, however, that the shift implied by Newman's thought is sufficient to dispel the carping of the cynics noted above. Newman did not believe that in doctrinal development he was arguing for that which was utterly new or innovative. We shall return to that theme a little later. The implication is rather than in the world that issued from Vatican II, theology and tradition began to be examined in the light of assumptions first enunciated by Newman, notably in his *Essay on the Development of Christian Doctrine*. To a large extent, pre-Vatican II Catholicism breathed a suffocating theological atmosphere; tradition was understood to be static and speculative thought was circumscribed. Some theologians, notably the Frenchmen Teilhard de Chardhin, Henri de Lubac and Yves Congar, had been prepared to swim against the tide, but they had had to pay for their sense of adventure. Indeed, two or three generations earlier, theologians had paid for their speculation more dearly still. The Catholic Modernists had been silenced by Papal Encyclical and prescriptive oaths.[3]

The significance of this negative view of change within Roman Catholicism, and its effects upon the place of religion within our culture, was felt well beyond the bounds of Catholicism and indeed of the institutional Church. Poet and novelist Thomas Hardy, well known for his scepticism about religion and the Church, regretted the suppression of the Catholic Modernists;

> ... the historic and once august hierarchy of Rome some genera-
> tion ago lost its chance of being the religion of the future by ...
> throwing over the little band of New Catholics who were
> making a struggle for continuity by applying the principle of
> evolution to their own faith, joining hands with modern science,
> and outflanking the hesitating English instinct towards liturgical
> restatement (a flank march which at the time I quite expected to
> witness, with the gathering of many millions into its fold).[4]

The implication of those moves within Roman Catholicism was one of a rigid and authoritarian view of Christian doctrine. Those who commented favourably on the theological legacy of the Second Vatican Council saw it as enshrining the implications of Newman's *Essay on the Development of Doctrine*, and as giving authority to the work of theologians who were writing under Newman's increasingly pervasive influence.

Anglicans have a particular interest in reflecting upon Newman and his work on the development of doctrine. The Tractarian movement had focused upon the nature of the Church and also on the formation of the tradition. Keble in his Assize Sermon of 1833 had attacked Erastianism, that is the confusion of the Church and secular government, and the subsequent implication of secular interference in the life of the Church. Keble and Newman both looked back to what they saw as an earlier purity within the Church, encapsulated within the writings of Patristic theologians. As the Tractarian movement developed its intellectual/theological reflection, so questions of the nature of the tradition, its development and formation became increasingly paramount to the discussion. The legacy which Newman's own writing in this area would leave would be significant for both the life and teaching of all mainstream Christian Churches thereafter. What then does it mean to say that Christian doctrine develops and in what might one seek the real identity of Christian belief?

Newman and the Development of Doctrine

Whether one can identify direct links between Newman's Essay and Vatican II is not central to our reflections here. What is undoubtedly true is that there is a consistency of approach in the historical consciousness exhibited both in Newman's Essay, and in the documents of the Second Vatican Council. It is this historical consciousness in our understanding of doctrine that is particularly germane to the subject matter of this book. Newman's theological perspicacity made it possible for this new historical consciousness to engage with a variety of philosophical and cultural questions hitherto unrelated. Owen Chadwick has placed Newman's work in context with both clarity and imagination.[5] Chadwick makes it clear that the problems broached by Newman in the *Essay* had been pinpointed by earlier writers, but often by accident and implication rather than by analysis.

The theologian Bossuet is a good example. Writing in the late seventeenth century on the historical continuity of Christian dogma, it is not clear that he did see the problem. When he referred to 'progress in doctrine', he simply referred to the progress of the gospel from land to land. Bossuet would have denied the profitability of doctrinal speculation and at the most would have accepted the unavoidability of debate to fend against heresy.[6] Some commentators even doubt whether he would have allowed that certain doctrines became more clearly defined later in the Church's history than they were in Patristic times. It does seem clear, however, in the work of other scholars (for example, the late seventeenth century scholars Mabillon and Tillemont,[7]) that there was a practical recognition of doctrinal change, without any theory yet being attached to it. Perceptions of Christian doctrine had now changed. It was no longer possible to say simplistically that 'what was good enough for St Paul is good enough for me', as it is alleged it was once said of the Authorised Version.

Owing to the growth of historical criticism as part of so-called Enlightenment thought, the world in which Newman found himself was a world now well accustomed to change, to the possibility of development in the history of ideas, and to the need to take human experience seriously. Critical history, empirical philosophy and modern science were developing apace. Apples fall to the ground, blood circulates in the human body, matter is composed of atoms; scientists utilised empirical observation to transform our thought world and our means of perception. Historians used documents to provide critical data – the German literary critics, Reimarus and Lessing, had applied this even to the Bible with devastating effect. Philosophers too were at pains to take sensory experience seriously. It would be easy to assume that Newman sat directly within the centre of this world of fermenting thought. Newman was no scientist, however, and he was not a student of German historiography, or even of liberal Anglican thought.[8] Nor indeed was his frame of mind predominantly philosophical, but rather historical.

On the contrary, it was the latitudinarianism of the age which set Newman and the other Tractarians off in search of sure and certain truths; they began by ransacking the doctrinal formularies of the Patristic world. They feared a relativising of the Christian tradition. Nevertheless, Newman's sensitivity was too great and his intelligence too acute to ignore the other factors we have noted which influenced the intellectual climate of his age. In other words, whilst Newman's essay was not the direct outflow of Darwinian evolution – we shall see that its flavour is quite different – it was, nevertheless, influenced by some of the intellectual breezes which would lead Darwin to his momentous thesis only fourteen years later. Furthermore, and here the *Essay on the Development of Doctrine* provides ample evidence of how the philosophical writings of Bishop Butler, with foundations reaching down to a firm basis in a theology based upon experience, were profoundly influential upon Newman's thought. This provides us with a map upon which we may locate the thought which became the raw material of Newman's momentous essay. What precisely, then, is the argument of his essay?

Paradoxically, the most crucial matter of all for John Henry Newman was that he should be able to prove the existence of continuity in Christian doctrine, notably within the Roman Catholic Church as he found it. It must be the same doctrine as had been imbibed by the apostles and Fathers of the Church. On this first level Newman stands foursquare with Bossuet and earlier writers and apologists and for very good reasons. Newman's own experience had led him gradually to see the Church of England as schismatic. Before he could accept the discipline of the Roman Catholic Church, however, he had to be persuaded of the real continuity of the Church of Rome in his day with the early Church. To this there were clearly many impediments and these he had explored in some detail and with great energy during his days within the Church of England. As he moved further along the path to Rome he needed to reassure himself of this crucial continuity. It was this that led to his writing the essay.

Continuity within Change?

The burden of Newman's argument is that if there are apparent accretions within Christian doctrine, then the seed for such luxuriant growths was there in the Church of the Early Fathers. At one point he states it thus:

> All surely will agree that these Fathers (St Athanasius and St Ambrose), with whatever differences of opinion, whatever protests, if we will, would find themselves more at home with such men as St Bernard or St Ignatius Loyola, or with the lonely priest in his lodgings or the holy sisterhood of mercy, or the unlettered crowd before the altar, than with the rulers of the members of any other religious community.[1]

This sort of purple passage appears on more than one occasion in his book. His point is that developments these may be, but 'true developments' are those now found in the Roman Catholic Church as he saw it. Much of his thesis is aimed at establishing tests for 'true developments' and thus distinguishing them from those which are false or rogue elements within Christian experience. Few would now defend the tests as effective or watertight means of making such distinctions although the question of what controls or defines the tradition remains significant. These tests remain, however, opportunities for Newman to attempt to build up his case that there is absolute continuity within Christian doctrine. In one of the most sonorous and memorable passages in the *Essay*, Newman puts it so:

> If there is a form of Christianity now in the world which is accused of gross superstition, or borrowing its rites and customs from the heathen, and of ascribing to forms and ceremonies an occult virtue; – a religion which (*and he continues to pile up a list of calumnious accusations against the Church of Rome until he reaches a conclusion rich in ironic hyperbole*) – if there be such a religion now in the world, it is not unlike Christianity as that same world viewed it, when first it came forth from its Divine Author.[10]

It is this affirmation of utter continuity which is the point of departure for Newman as he sets out on his journey at the beginning of his *Essay*.[11] Very early on, he uses the so-called Vincentian Canon: '*Quod semper, quod ubique, quod ab omnibus*' (what has been held always, everywhere, and by all) to describe Christian continuity, and this dictum re-appears in 'rondo' form throughout the rest of the essay. Newman is keen not to be thought of at any stage as latitudinarian that is, unconcerned with dogmatic truth or ecclesiastical organisation, in his tendencies. Indeed, it was against such tendencies that he was writing. This was a disease well exemplified for him in people like Thomas Arnold and Dr Hampden, with whom he came into contact while still a fellow Anglican. He spills much ink in establishing the importance of continuity in Christian belief.

If, however, his concern to see himself as within the same Church as the apostles was a controlling element within his argument, so his real appreciation of change was what had forced him both to reflect upon and write about the development of doctrine. This realisation was to occasion one of the most quoted aphorisms within the *Essay*, when he wrote: 'In a higher world it is otherwise; but here below to live is to change and to be perfect is to change often.[12] Even so, Newman was still careful to preserve the continuity which he had argued so strenuously for with the support of the Vincentian Canon. It is at this point that both his reliance upon and his divergence from Bishop Butler becomes most manifest. In a University Sermon at one point he notes: 'Butler is speaking of the discovery of new truths in passages of Scripture, and the text speaks of a further insight into the primitive and received sense of scripture passages, gained by meditating upon them and bringing out their own idea more completely.'[13] Newman is keen to distinguish the process of discovering new truths from ancient texts from the discovery of further insights into ancient truths. This particular part of the argument was essential to Newman both intellectually and thus by implication existentially, if he was to make the move into the Roman Catholic Church. We need constantly to remind ourselves that the *Essay* is effectively a justification of Newman's conversion to Roman Catholicism, written as he contemplated making such a move.

Newman's *Essay* was, however, more than simply the justification for the personal action of one individual. In analysing the problem for himself, Newman saw the crucial nature of the questions raised for the whole Church of God. In what sense could continuity be preserved whilst taking seriously the very obvious elements of change? So, for example, this impinges very sharply with regard to Christianity's relationship with other religions and philosophies. He makes it clear that from the beginning there was a 'cardinal distinction between Christianity and the religions and philosophies by which it was surrounded. By keeping fixed principles, Christianity has been able to incorporate doctrine which was external to it without losing its own.'[14] Christian doctrine is thus not 'infected' by its surrounding culture. Instead the seeds which are there within it from the start are assisted in flowering, through surrounding religions and philosophies, only where these same seeds lie hidden within Christianity from its inception. There is no grafting on of foreign growths or parasitical organisms. In this process of assimilation, as Newman designates it, the Church takes in doctrines from outside, transmuting them for her own purposes. Newman thus argues very strongly for change and continuity. Indeed, the extraordinary power with which Newman argues both for change and continuity identified him as a nineteenth century precursor of that method which our twentieth century cynic noted when he wrote of the one who: '... spends many years discovering a new insight and then just as many years proving that it is not really new.'[15]

Doctrine – an Unfolding Flower

To leave the discussion at this point, however, would be to do a grave injustice both to the intelligence and originality of Newman's thesis. Roman Catholicism certainly had been unable to conceive of any sense in which there might be a progression of any sort in doctrine, other than its spread to new shores and other climes. Anything more than this would smack of dallying with heresy or entertaining the possibility of the corruptibility of doctrine. Both these possibilities were unacceptable to Newman but he could see quite clearly that change had occurred. To use a human analogy, Newman saw the process as a stage within the gradual maturing of Christian understanding, a move towards healthy adulthood. Christian doctrine was not corruptible, but neither was it manifested in its fullness from the beginning. Doctrines were either there in an embryonic form, gradually developing until they burst forth into flower, or, on other occasions, there was nothing at all to be seen on the surface of the Christian plant, not even a bud. Hidden, however, within the organism lay the seeds of other doctrines which must appear if the organism as a whole is to assume the appearance of mature adulthood. Newman states it thus:

> Here we see the difference between originality of mind and the gift and calling of a Doctor in the Church; the holy fathers just mentioned were intently fixing their minds on what they taught, grasping it more and more closely, viewing it on various sides, trying its consistency, weighing their own separate expressions. And thus if in some cases they were even left in ignorance, the next generation of teachers completed their work, for the same unwearied anxious process of thought went on.[16]

Newman thus brought together two particularly significant elements in forging his theory of development. The first was that acute sense of history which had allied him with Edward Bouverie Pusey and John Keble as they had led together the Oxford movement in Newman's days as an Anglican. His sense of history taught him both how the contemporary Roman Church differed from the Church of the Fathers, but also how important was the authority of that historic Church. Hence it led him directly on to the second most significant element in his theory, that being the central place of the authority of the Church in guarding the continuity of doctrine. This was the means by which the church retained what Newman called its 'fixed principles'. It is the conjunction, then, of these two elements that give to Newman's *Essay* its tantalising combination of innovation and a more static affirmation of the tradition.

Despite his original intentions, both as a Tractarian and then in his move to the Roman Communion, of seeking out the primitive and continuing elements of the Christian gospel, it fell to Newman to be the discoverer of the historically conditioned nature of Christian dogma. Newman was undoubtedly one of those chiefly responsible for introducing to the Church the notion of 'historical consciousness' in its understanding of Christian doctrine. The other side of the coin, however, is Newman's determination to hold on to continuity and to the Church's tradition, its fixed principles. It is thus inadequate either to see the *Essay* as an excursion into liberalism, or as being untouched by the emerging critical tools of the age. So Chadwick writes: 'That Newman's theory of development was not a liberal theory, in the sense of contemporary evolutionary philosophy, is certain. But that his expression of it was influenced by the continental school of history whose influence was rising all around him is to my mind equally certain.' [17] The movements of thought which are generally given the label of the Enlightenment, as a shorthand, unavoidably coloured Newman's work.

The result of the tension in Newman's thought here described is to place upon his understanding of the development of Christian doctrine a static influence. Admittedly, Newman had not only recognised change, he had also justified and explained it. He was still concerned, however, that there should be some means of controlling that change and keeping it within certain acceptable limits. The 'tests' were an attempt at providing these limits. While the tests themselves may fail to convince, it is still the case that Newman is capable of producing a thesis where the doctrinal development discerned appears to be the only possible development that could have happened. An invisible hand (attributed by Newman to the authority of the Church) has preserved

Christianity in truth. The truth as now stated was predetermined from the earliest days. Not only are incarnation, Trinity, and sacramental theology consistent with the thought of the Fathers, their contemporary theological exposition could not have turned out in any other way. They were the necessary development of the earliest tradition. As we shall argue in the next chapter, however, it is not clear that this satisfies the intellectual questions it seeks to answer. Newman bequeathed to Christian theology a historical consciousness, but with ecclesiastical strings attached.

Inevitability and Change

How can this fit into a picture of enlightenment thought seen as a self contained phenomenon? Suffice to say that it is inadequate to see the enlightenment as a discrete two or even three hundred year phenomenon. Instead it must be seen as part of a process which has now spanned some five centuries at least but which probably reaches back further still into the later middle ages. Its roots lie in the twelfth century renaissance, in the fifteenth century roots of modern science, and in the long term development of the Western intellectual tradition. Newman and those who have followed are not the helpless victims of the fashions or even whims of a passing age. Instead they are situated on a wider canvas set in the context of a complex and gradually developing pattern of European thought within which at certain points may be discerned evolutionary 'leaps' in understanding. Even progress in Christian doctrine as a specific issue has roots stretching down well below the ground on which Newman found himself.[18] The growth of empiricism seen in the development of modern science, in empirical philosophy and in critical history leaves its mark upon Newman's thesis. Furthermore, the very process of doctrinal development itself becomes clearer and more conspicuous once this empirical approach to intellectual endeavour has gained a firm hold. Catholicism has not been the lone victim of such spontaneous growth; Protestant theology and practice has been formed by similar influences. Newman could, of course, see this. His own experience had encompassed other forms of development in Anglicanism. He was keen to point out in the *Essay* that if there was continuity with the Church of the Fathers, then it was continuity with the Roman Catholicism available to Newman, and not with what he now saw as the more spurious developments within Anglicanism or the Protestant churches.

It may also be the case that the growing tide of positivism and even determinism, often seen to be the enemy of religion, helped strengthen Newman's particular view of development. Newman knew the necessity for continuity and the reality of change. To preserve the Church in truth, authority must legislate for an inevitable pattern of development. How else could heresy be shunned and orthodoxy prosper? This meant that the plants now flourishing, the developments now observed and practised in the life of the Church, (that is the Roman Catholic Church), had to be seen as the only possible developments, bearing in mind the nature of the primaeval seeds. 'The argument was futile unless the full flower of developed doctrine was "anticipated" by a bud which you could see – by scraps of indubitable information.' [19] Such arguments would be paralleled in some of the deterministic science of the later nineteenth century and perhaps most clearly of all in the determinism of the infant human sciences of economics, psychology and sociology.

Marx, Freud, Durkheim and Weber all took their turn in contributing towards different types of humanistic determinism. Nevertheless, if such influences, in embryo, bore upon Newman and his world, then so too did the legacy of classical theism. One ought not to be surprised that the pattern of doctrinal development appeared to unfold to a preset and unalterable code. It could be seen as virtually an extension of the omniscience of the deity himself. God knew the course of all history and thought from the beginning of time and here we see it unfolding upon the stage of human experience. In the development of doctrine was captured a concrete realisation of what had been there since the inception of Creation in the mind of God. To capitalise upon a scientific analogy which we shall develop later, the process can be compared to contemporary theories of reproduction in living species. The theory of evolution, when combined with discoveries in genetics, assumes that in the vast majority of cases, reproduction results in exact replication of the cells and thus of the species. In a very small, but nevertheless significant, number of cases an error or mutation occurs. When this mutation survives and itself replicates, so an evolutionary leap takes place. Newman's theory of development corresponds to this theory, robbed of the errors which lead to mutations and change. The pattern is there in the DNA and it replicates itself inexorably and with no possibility of error or corruption. So it is with Christian doctrine; it had to be this way, that is predetermined in the apostolic truth.

This description of Newman's work on development could easily be perceived as *ungenerous* and highlighting only its inadequacies. Certainly there remain in Newman unresolved tensions which relate partly to his own dilemma and partly to the religious culture of nineteenth century Roman Catholicism. In the light of subsequent developments, elements of Newman's theory are bound to be intellectually unsatisfying. To deny this is to deny one's own historical consciousness. Newman's theory instead must be set against the wider canvas of the development of European thought, and specifically the development of theological thought. Seen within that context it is insufficient to describe the *Essay* as a by-product of evolutionary philosophy or indeed as part of the enlightenment phenomenon. The danger with such an appreciation is that it can allow us either to dismiss it as an intellectual 'erratic' upon a wider and more extensive plain, or to raise it to the top of a theological pantheon, there to stand beyond criticism. Instead, having seen the enlightenment itself (and evolutionary thought within the so-called enlightenment period) to be part of a far longer and more complex pattern of intellectual development, we are allowed to see Newman's *Essay* as one stage along a continuing journey. Newman's observation of doctrinal change and his attempted justification of it was a momentous breakthrough and leap forward in our appreciation of the development of Christian thought. Released from an unrealistic incarceration in the thought-patterns of either the Counter-Reformation or antiquity, Christian theologians could breathe a more bracing air. That Christian doctrine did change and must change was both accepted and affirmed. A new realism is made possible through Newman's work. Did not this now establish that the faith of our Fathers had moved unmistakably into the atmosphere of healthy maturity, where doctrine was in full flower?

The setting of Newman's work within the wider context of historical consciousness has led us to have hesitations about this final assertion. These hesitations relate to the concept of healthy adulthood, full flower, that is a final and irreformable pattern of doctrine. Does Newman's *Essay* remain a final and adequate analysis of the phenomenon of doctrinal development, or are the tensions which remain unresolved in his work the signals for us to continue with further attempts at understanding the nature of our faith? Posing this question in a slightly different form, is the process of 'inevitable development' described by Newman still supported by the historical and theological evidence available to us? Perhaps the only effective means of answering this question is to examine one doctrine in the light of his thesis and see whether the results are consistent with experience and provide intellectual satisfaction. Historical consciousness and empirical method both call for a worked example.

Chapter 2

Revisiting Christian Belief

Tradition or Development?

My first childhood holiday at Littlehampton was, I think at the age of eight. It was a childhood paradise – sandy beach, a small fairground, an impressive river estuary with lots of yachting, 'Punch and Judy' shows, and all the rest. We revisited that same town for our summer holidays in the following two years and each time stayed for three weeks. It was all firmly imprinted in my infant mind. My next visit was not until 21 years later. So well had I known it, that photographic images of the town remained with me as we approached it now with my own family. The impact of this visit was very sharp indeed. Not only did the town fail to live up to my romantic memories, there was even a disjunction in the lie of the land. Buildings and roads seemed to be relocated, colours had faded, and the gloss had gone. It wasn't simply that everything looked so much smaller, a phenomenon known to all of us on revisiting childhood haunts, it was actually different. Of course, I ought not to have been surprised. To begin with, my perception had developed. I now saw things differently. Values had changed – that which had been exciting or colourful now looked tasteless or even gaudy. Buildings which had seemed elegant or impressive now felt commonplace. But it was not simply my changed perception and world view, important as these were. The place itself had also changed. Relief roads had cut swathes through the little town. Buildings had been demolished, and others had been put up in their place. Even the exciting swing-bridge had given way to the functional fixed concrete arc which now leaps across the river to the north of the town. All this took a good deal of absorbing, and I suspect some of it will never fully enter my system. The childhood images will remain.

At a deeper level, psychotherapists and psychologists often encourage us to rediscover or revisit our childhood. Through recapitulation of those experiences our present perceptions and responses may be changed. Opinions may differ on the effectiveness of such therapy. Unanimity, however, would exist on the fact that perceptions change from childhood as we move toward maturity. To rediscover our roots, to revisit our past, is almost certain to be educationally enriching. How much can similar reflections to these, which each of us could contribute, illuminate our understanding of Christian faith and the way it is formulated? What might it mean to revisit doctrine, or even one particular doctrine? Some would argue that no parallel exists. After all, Christianity is an historical religion and historical facts cannot change like buildings and by-passes. That, however, takes us very little further forward. The facts upon which faith is based are now difficult to recover, in any precise manner. Admittedly few would question the fact of Jesus' life on this earth, and the vast majority accept the fact of his crucifixion. Beyond that, however, lies the world of interpretation, and such is the raw material of doctrine. Atonement, eschatology and resurrection are ground fertile for discussion. They are not brute facts.

Tradition or Development

This has been pressed home vividly in recent controversies. A statement from the House of Bishops of the Church of England[1] attempted to address such issues. Such was the heat generated by these questions that even a *Times'* leader focused on the question 'Can Doctrine Develop?'[2] Almost 150 years after John Henry Newman's *Essay on the Development* many would be surprised that such a question could even be asked. Of course doctrine can develop. Our earlier reflections demonstrated how Newman arrived at his theory and how it issued from broader patterns of thought at the time. The *Times'* editorial seemed less certain of Newman's conclusions, however, and noted: 'So an alternative dividing line down which Christianity may yet split is between those who believe in the possibility of the development of doctrine, and those who do not. ... Such a division would ... have surprising results: it would put the Roman Catholic Church in the same (pro-development) camp as the movement for the Ordination of Women, with the Bishop of London standing with the Orthodox churches and Protestant fundamentalists.'[3]

Although this smacks of journalistic polemic, the importance of the question cannot be ignored, for ultimately it relates to the identity and continuity of the Christian community. Who are the true heirs of the Christian spirit, the developmentalists or the 'traditionalists'? The question is very sharp indeed.

As we have seen, Newman's picture of doctrinal development is highly controlled, and indeed the aim of his thesis in its original conception was very conservative. How could Christianity continue as one phenomenon when clearly the Church and many of its beliefs were very different from the beliefs of the apostles and the early Fathers? Newman's answer was to develop an image of doctrine as a flower unfolding. Revisit the garden and the same flower will be there but more of it will be visible each time we return. From the bud bursts forth a dazzling array of petals. At one point in his thesis Newman uses a scriptural analogy:

> Lastly, while scripture nowhere recognises itself, or asserts the inspiration of these portions which are most essential, it distinctly anticipates the development of Christianity, both as polity and as a doctrine. In one of our Lord's parables 'The Kingdom of Heaven' is even compared to a 'grain of mustard seed which a man took and hid in his field; which is indeed the least of all seeds, but when it is grown it is the greatest among herbs, and becometh a tree ...'[4]

The potential had been there all along. Newman simply – or rather not so simply – sets out clear criteria to distinguish true from false developments.

The compulsion of Newman's argument in its essence is undeniable, since it is based on empirical observation of change in Christian doctrine. This undoubtedly led to the suspicious and ambivalent response of Roman Catholics in the nineteenth century to the man who was certainly intellectually their most able English convert. Since then the cultural winds which bore Newman on the road towards his doctrine of development have not abated, but rather increased. The gathering forces of the Enlightenment, which made his analysis possible have further heightened historical awareness. Sociological relativism has brought more tempestuous weather still. This, together with the religious pluralism of western society, has made the inevitability of the particular stream of development implied in Newman's thesis less than obvious. In spite of his argument, it could have been otherwise, even within the embryonic Christian community. For example, the concept of *agape* may be common to a number of writers, but its meaning varies enormously and because of this a number of different ethical thrusts are implied by the different documents. This is clear from scripture. So the Johannine letters have an exclusive notion of the concept of *agape*, the Greek word used in the New Testament for disinterested love. (See 1. John 4.7 ff and elsewhere in the three letters). The implications in Luke, however, for the living out of the gospel message are very different, as we can note in the inclusiveness of the teaching in the parable of the Good Samaritan (Luke 10.25–37). The Pauline 'hymn to love' (1. Cor. 13) fills out the concept of *agape* in yet different terms again.

All these arguments suggest that in revisiting doctrine, the concept of development, as it has come to be understood, may now be inadequate. Do we need to seek out a different image or model which more accurately describes the process uncovered through a still more sophisticated appreciation of historical consciousness?

The Trinity: Development or Evolution?

To begin to answer that question we can do no better than to make a number of fleeting visits to a particular dogma in the course of its history. Ultimately it matters little which doctrine we choose for our worked example, although it may help to pick on a dogma that has a long and prestigious history which on earlier assessments has been seen to have developed in a predictable manner. The obvious candidate is Trinitarian belief.

If we begin with the New Testament, we can claim virtually universal agreement that there is no developed doctrine of the Trinity within its pages. Even the most conservative proponents of Trinitarian thought are prepared to admit as much.[5] Of course, there are points where Trinitarian formulae are quoted, notably at the end of Matthew's gospel in the command to baptise, 'Therefore go and make disciples of all the nations, baptising them in the name of the Father and of the Son and of the Holy Spirit.' (Matthew 28.19). A similar formula is there also in the Pauline grace on one occasion 'May the grace of the Lord Jesus Christ, and the love of God and the fellowship of the Holy Spirit be with you all.' (2. Cor. 13.14). Elsewhere, however, Paul himself is happy to allow his grace to refer back only to Jesus or to refer to only two persons within the Godhead 'Grace and peace to you from God our Father and the Lord Jesus Christ.' (2. Cor. 1.2). Discussion of the development of Trinitarian thought necessitates, however, a far deeper analysis of the New Testament than simply reflection upon formulae. If the notion of an essential Trinity, that is a Trinity which actually describes the relationships within the Godhead, is to be supported then a clear picture of the co-equality of the Son with the Father must be argued, and indeed alongside that a developed doctrine of the Spirit. Even with the first of these tasks we are in some considerable difficulty. Some commentators note that nowhere in the New Testament is the full co-equality of the Son implied, in what we would now understand as standard incarnational terminology. Putting this position on one side, it cannot be denied that there is a great variety of different doctrinal formulations of the relationship of Jesus to the Father within the New Testament. The writings of one New Testament author alone include variation. Take for example the hymn, probably pre-Pauline, used in Colossians 1.15–19:

> He is the image of the invisible God, the firstborn of all creation.
> For by him all things were created; things in heaven and on earth, visible and invisible, whether thrones or powers or rulers or authorities; all things were created by him and for him. He is before all things, and in him all things hold together. And he is the head of the body, the church; he is the beginning, the

firstborn from among the dead, so that in everything he might have the supremacy. For God was pleased to have all his fulness dwell in him, and through him to reconcile to himself all things ...

This clearly depicts Jesus as pre-existent (i.e. existing prior to his conception in Mary's womb) in a manner similar to that in John 1.1. 'In the beginning was the Word, and the Word was with God, and the Word was God.' In Romans 1, Jesus is spoken of in such a way as to imply that he only became God's son after his earthly life, a kind of Christology often described as 'Adoptionist': '... who as to his human nature was a descendant of David, and who through the Spirit of holiness was declared with power to be the Son of God, by his resurrection from the dead ...' This is very different from the vision of Colossians.

Examples could be multiplied and numerous different theses have been propounded in recent years in monographs specifically concerned with New Testament Christology.[6] The burden of the argument so far is that there is an undeniable pluralism in the New Testament writings on basic christological doctrine. A similar argument could be set out in relation to the doctrine of the Spirit, although here the evidence is more sparse and less developed than with the christological material. Certainly there are references to the coming of the Spirit in John's gospel and also in the accounts of the early church in the Acts of the Apostles. (John 14.15; Acts 2.1–13). What is in dispute, however, is whether we are here reading simply of different types of reference to the indwelling and continuing presence of Christ, or whether the references are to a further divine hypostasis, that is person within the Godhead, as envisaged in later Patristic Trinitarian doctrine. The result of such investigation is the discovery of great variety. It is difficult to see any of this as obviously convergent, or manifesting a unified development which implies an incipient Trinitarianism. Instead, the picture is of a number of parallel processes taking place which issue in sometimes radically different and opposed conclusions. Each process relates to the situation and needs of the individual church, and to some extent to the thought patterns in which the deliberations of each separate writer were clothed. The infant Church and the early Fathers were the inheritors of a very mixed tradition.

In an exhaustive analysis of the growth of Trinitarian Christianity, it would be important to trace the complex movements of thought in the realm of christology. In this brief sketch, however, it will suffice to move directly from the New Testament background to the fourth century, where in a comparatively short space of time Trinitarian doctrine grew into what became known as orthodoxy. Commentators following in the tradition of the Reformed theologian Karl Barth, to whom we shall return in a later chapter, have seen this as the crucial point in the development of what is now regarded as orthodox Christian belief. Rooting their argument in a radical christological basis for the Trinity, the Councils of Nicaea and Constantinople of AD 325 and 381 are then seen as precluding the possibility or indeed the necessity for any further development or change in doctrine from that point onward. In a recent monograph on Trinitarian belief, Thomas Torrance, a notable exponent of this school, goes as far as to assert: 'Hence it came about that the Nicene Council expressed the fundamental beliefs which were found to be evangelically compelling in a Creed which has subsequently been universally acknowledged in the Church, and which by its intrinsic structure excludes alternative doctrine as arbitrary innovation in face of God's one self-revelation in Jesus Christ, i.e. as heretical deviation from the truth.'[7] His argument is for a givenness within Trinitarian doctrine which issues from the Nicene-Constantinopolitan document. It is not clear, however, that this is supportable in the face of historical critical study of the background to the production of these documents. The beginnings of the formulation of Trinitarian belief lay rather in the background of the Arian controversy and thus admittedly in a different sense in christological developments. Indeed, James Mackey argues that: 'The Christian doctrine of the Trinity is properly speaking a christological doctrine, that is not at all a doctrine about God before or independently of the revelation (for those who take it as such) in Jesus.[8] Even those who are substantially critical of Mackey's work are prepared to concede that this reflects the attitudes and perhaps even the experience of the majority of Christians within the western tradition.

Unitarianism or Tri-theism?

Accepting this is to be the case, wherein lay the difficulty that fuelled the protracted controversy between Athanasius and Arius? The essence of the divide between the two protagonists takes us as far back as the position represented by a number of thinkers of the third century, the best known of whom was Sabellius (a theologian probably writing from Rome of whom little is known). Sabellius was principally concerned to preserve the unity of the Godhead and was thus unhappy about talk of the fullness of three persons. Instead he wished to allow God only to relate to his creation in three different modalities, rather than existing as three differentiated persons. The obvious danger here was that the Son was seen simply as emanating from the Father. Father and Son, using this approach, are not thought of as distinct hypostases (as we have noted, the technical term used for 'persons' used by the Church Fathers) but only as different modes of the divine person. This doctrine was therefore called 'modalism' and sometimes 'Monarchian modalism', because the Son and the Spirit were subsumed under the dominant person of the Father, or primal Godhead.

Arius is often accused of lapsing into a similar error by extending back the pre-existence of Christ so as to preserve the immutability of God. In doing so, however, it is argued he did nothing to amend the subordinationist pictures of Christ prevalent at the time.[9] The Son was less than the Father. The result of this picture is another emanationist view of Christ which falls short of the *homoousios* formula which declared that Son and Father are 'of the same substance', and thus equal within the Godhead. The Son again is not clearly established as a distinct hypostasis. While the evidence for this view is considerable,[10] there is also contrary evidence to suggest that Arius' failure was not in an insufficient discrimination of divine substance. Instead the opposite was true. His was a sharp clarity. He required the Son to fall on the human side of the divide. This divide was produced by the differentiation required by a doctrine of *creatio ex nihilo*[11], that is, creation out of nothing. Either way the Son becomes subordinate; he is not co-equal with the Father.

Whichever of these two interpretations of the evidence we accept, it is far from obvious that the triumphant solution was the obvious result of a clear line of development. Indeed the existence of two such different lines of interpretation emphasise this point further. Admittedly, in his argument, Mackey is criticised by other theologians for producing over-sharp disjunctions in the patristic material which are based upon a presupposed conclusion.[12] Although this criticism may have some substance, it is hard to accept the conclusion that the homoousiite formula was the necessary and inevitable result of three hundred years of development, as some seem to imply. The Athanasian formula agreed at Nicaea has an innovative, even a revolutionary feel about it. Whether emanationism or *creatio ex nihilo* motivated Arius, he was clearly primarily concerned to preserve a mono-theistic model of God. The triumphant Athanasian doctrine propounded a radically new picture where the preservation of the unity of the Godhead was less of a foregone con-clusion. Arius' argument may have been too clear-cut, but he could see only too sharply the other dangers that loomed beneath the patristic mists. Although the details of his argu-ment have become a matter of history, his way of thinking has re-surfaced from time to time in the Church's history, as in the thought of the sixteenth century Italian theologian Socinus, in Arminianism and the so-called Anglican Arians of the eighteenth century. More recently linguistic philo-sophy has been used to deliver a fresh critique of the Nicene formula that the Son is 'of the same substance' (or 'one in Being' as the revised English version of the Creed has it). From this point of view the question is not whether the formula is a true representation of how things are in the inner being of God but of whether the formula makes logical sense.

This, however, is not the point of our argument. Instead we are concerned about the nature of the move which was agreed at Nicaea. Rather than it being a natural and inevitable development, historical analysis suggests that it was a more revolutionary shift in perception than it now appears, when we see it as part of mainstream orthodox Christian doctrine. Trinitarianism attempted to answer the question: 'How could the unity of the Godhead be preserved at the same time as giving equal honour to Father and Son?' Using a scientific analogy, a Copernican revolution had taken place which, viewed from a historical perspective, cannot be seen as inevitable, or indeed as the only possible solution, nor indeed can it be seen as the 'given' form implied by Torrance and others, the only possible conclusion of an inevitable process.

Embracing the Spirit

Further evidence for a revolutionary break at Nicaea is gathered from the continued controversies in the years which followed the council. The work of Maurice Wiles and other 'doctrinal critics' has led us to see this against the background of contemporary cultural and political pressures. We should not expect such a sharp disjunction in thought patterns to be swallowed immediately by an entire culture, especially in the volatile world of fourth century imperial politics.

If we accept the revolutionary Copernican nature of the solution adopted by the Nicene Fathers, then the next stage in the history of the growth of Trinitarian thought may, at first sight, appear to be obviously developmental. This next stage is effectively the work of the Cappadocian Fathers (St Basil of Caesarea, his brother St Gregory of Nyssa and St Gregory Nazianzus) in moving the formula on from one of agreement on the Father and the Son to the Trinitarian Chalcedonian Definition of 381. The apparent inevitability of this move issues from the fact that Christians had since New Testament times spoken of God as Father, Son and Spirit and the place of the Holy Spirit within the Godhead had not been disputed, although it had not been the subject of careful theological discussion. The Cappadocians began from this assumption and their development of the final stages of Trinitarianism issued from the Church's life of worship and prayer. In this sense, this stage in the growth of

Trinitarian doctrine issued from very different roots to its predecessor. Nevertheless similar philosophical presuppositions underpinned both moves. In including the Spirit, the Cappadocians were determined to reclaim the unity of Godhead which some felt had been threatened. This they achieved by emphasising the unity of divine activity. All three persons of the Trinity act co-equally and, so concurrently, thus we cannot differentiate the three persons functionally through their activity in the world.[13] Instead, the three persons are distinguished on the basis of the Cappadocians' radical Platonist conception of deity. Hence Gregory of Nazianzus differentiates using the concepts of ingeneracy, generation and procession, and Gregory of Nyssa uses concepts based on causality.[14] Contemporary difficulties in using these philosophical categories, are compounded by an epistemological difficulty. In other words, how can we come to know of this distinction within the divine life without it relating to our own religious experience, or that of others? [15]

It would be to digress to pursue these particular problems any further at this point, however. What should be clear is that we have uncovered another disjunction in the growth of Trinitarian belief. Whilst it may appear clear to us in retrospect that the resolution of the Arian controversy at Nicaea should be followed by inclusion of the Spirit, it was not historically or theologically inevitable that Trinitarian development should have taken the turn which it did. First of all there is a distinct sense in which this new stage of growth issued from the twin impulses of spirituality and experience, which is less obviously true of the previous phase of growth. Secondly, the radical Platonist concepts employed deny these very experiential roots which had been the seed-bed for growth. Both of these complications tell against any inevitable *doctrinal development* in the generally accepted sense of the word. Here is no flower unfolding in an expected and pre-determined way.

Modern Developments

We shall now make an enormous leap from the fourth century to the Enlightenment (conceived in the terms of our earlier description, that is extending it back into the earlier history of the development of the European intellectual tradition) and to the conclusions which have issued from that lengthy and complex movement of thought. This leap is justified since this later period produced the next major shift in thinking on Trinitarian doctrine after the finalisation of orthodox belief in the Chalcedonian Definition. Indeed, those same philosophical and historical developments have made possible the analysis in which we have just been engaged. Positive growth in theological understanding has also ensued during this period. Almost certainly the crucial figure in this theological flowering has been Friedrich Schleiermacher, who, in his monumental study of religion and self-consciousness, firmly places the locus of theological study back in the realm of religious experience. In doing so, he also takes seriously the significance of the Church. If all western philosophy is in some sense footnotes to Plato, as Whitehead whimsically noted, then much western critical theology now reads as footnotes to Schleiermacher.

In the realm of Trinitarian discourse, theology post-Schleiermacher has re-opened the case for a different understanding of the Christian concept of God. In this country alone, a number of essays have questioned the viability of *essential* trinitarianism,[16] that view of God as Trinity which assumes that we can have knowledge of the nature of relationships between the persons within the Godhead and that the different persons of the Trinity are not purely 'modalities' of God's dealings with humanity. Much of this discussion was brought together in a rigorous and comprehensive form in Geoffrey Lampe's Bampton Lectures[17] and more recently still in the work previously cited by James Mackey.[18] Geoffrey Lampe's argument issues from a sustained discussion of the early Church Fathers with regard to the development of both a clear understanding of the nature of Christ's divinity and also the personhood of the Holy Spirit. Lampe is exercised by concepts of pre-existence. How can we now understand the Greek philosophical concepts which came to describe Jesus as pre-existing in God before his earthly life? He writes: 'According to this Christology, the eternal Son assumes a timeless human nature, or makes it timeless by making it his own; it is a human nature which owes nothing essential to geographical circumstances; it corresponds to nothing in the actual concrete world; Jesus Christ has not, after all, really "come in the flesh".' [19]

Lampe further points to the profound metaphysical problems that were raised, notably in the work of the Cappadocian Fathers, by the assertion that the Holy Spirit is a separate divine hypostasis. His answer to these problems is to argue for an understanding of God as Spirit. Incarnation does not disappear, but the classical Chalcedonian formula describing the nature of Christ is no longer an accurate summary of Trinitarian faith as Lampe would state it. An economic Trinity (that is, a Trinity in which God is active in different *modes*) is one possible description of Lampe's position. Some would argue it produces a form of binitarianism. Mackey too argues for a form of economic Trinity, following a critical discussion of traditional formulae. For him, the impulses which lead us to doctrinal affirmations are rather those of religious experience. This produces for Mackey an understanding of God's different modes of activity in relatively similar terms to those of Lampe. [20] The burden of both their arguments, it is suggested, move us in the direction of some form of unitarian or at least binitarian belief. The Son and the Spirit lose their distinctive identity as persons within the Godhead. God acts at different moments in different modalities which human experience describes as Father, Son or Spirit. Nevertheless terms like Binitarianism or Unitarianism themselves are unhelpful since they often act as labels and slogans rather than precise theological definitions. It is better to avoid such terms and instead realise that the arguments expounded by Lampe and others do not exclude differentiation in our perception of divine activity. Rather they question both the logic and the possibility of our knowing anything in detail of distinctions within the life of the Godhead. These conclusions have not passed without criticism.

David Brown, Van Mildert Professor of Divinity in the University of Durham, is critical of such 1970s' liberals as Wiles and Lampe. His own work on the Trinity [21] seeks to reconstruct Trinitarian doctrine by criticising what he calls 'non-interventionist' views of God and calling for a greater emphasis on and analysis of religious experience. Brown's critique begins from a philosophical standpoint with regard to God's dealings with his creation. His discussion touches on issues which have been long debated, centring on a need for God to intervene in this world. His criticism of much liberal theology is that in attempts to preserve human free will and indeed to demythologise our understanding of atonement, God appears to have little direct relationship with the created order. What is God doing all the time? This debate relates, of course, to wider questions of providence and theodicy. Brown, however, uses the term providence in a narrower sense to describe God's activity in the Incarnation and in the person of the Holy Spirit. This is the 'essential' foundation upon which he wishes to base a reaffirmation of classical Trinitarian faith. He writes sharply in his first chapter: '... if there is to be a proper incarnation, God the Son cannot stand aloof from the created order but must become interrelated with it, in a reciprocal exchange with a particular aspect of it ...'[22] It is far from clear, however, that Brown is successful in reclaiming the ground he seeks to reclaim. His thesis may achieve both too little and too much. In attempting to avoid crude interventionism, he gives away much of the ground he is trying to reclaim. His interventionism coincides with many of the facets of the non-interventionism which he attacks. He is all too aware of the dangers of naiveté when talking of God's activity in the world and so he does not appeal to the miraculous, nor does he believe that God ever imposes a particular viewpoint upon a human agent. Furthermore he tends to identify his model of God as Trinity and then to seek evidence for this from the New Testament. His attempt to buttress his argument with support from scripture is unconvincing. In Brown's account, the divine persons still feel as if they are well distanced from the earth; only the Son has any real relationship with that which God has created. The result is an exaggerated transcendence; God is further away from the world. This is affirmed at the expense of a real affirmation of God's immanence in his creation.

Starting from Prayer

This danger is pointed out sharply by one of Brown's most cogent critics, Sarah Coakley, who is equally unconvinced by Mackey's argument from experience. Her objection to Mackey is that he cannot allow God to be both united and differentiated. He cannot allow Trinity and unity to live together in God. As with Lampe, Mackey's argument is that our encounter with God through the historical Jesus is again with God as spirit. Coakley points to yet another way forward. Her argument is first 'that not every element of Christian truth can be necessarily found in clear form in the "faith of Jesus".'[23] This is an implicit criticism of Mackey and others which she makes explicit earlier on in her article. It suggests that all too easily critical scholarship opts for a revised form of nineteenth century Liberal Protestantism. In such approaches, all is concentrated on an (admittedly modest) picture of the *historical* Jesus and what he taught.[24] It may be right to accept this modest picture of Jesus. We must also be clear, however, that numerous 'authentic' responses to the impulse which Jesus initiated have existed in the community which has followed him. It is just one of these responses that Coakley seizes upon. She roots the doctrine of the Trinity in human experience, and notably in silent prayer, with a particular stress on the mystical tradition. She talks of a divine reflexivity, of God praying in us, and of this adverting us to a richer experience of God than simply that of 'a distant and undifferentiated divine entity'. Coakley's argument also owes a particular debt to Paul, notably in Romans 8.26f and 1. Cor. 12.3. Starting from this point, she suggests that 'the Spirit's distinctive workings in prayer may bring about in the pray-er an enormously enlarged understanding of what we mean by "Christ", an understanding both broader and deeper than any assessment of the "historical evidence".'[25] In a different context where one suspects that the argument owes its origins and form to the work of Coakley, it is made clear that such an approach to Trinitarian doctrine is not purely individualistic. The argument runs:

> Although concern with prayer experience may at first sight reflect a peculiarly modern obsession with direct personal authentica-

tion (and indeed carry with it dangers of a kind of narcissistic introversion), nonetheless sustained prayer leads rather to the building up of community than to its dissolution, to intensification rather than atrophy of concern for the life of the world.[26]

Her argument is attractive and subtle, and the abiding picture at the end of her discussion is religiously nourishing as well as theologically coherent. Her ability, even in these tantalisingly short paragraphs to call witnesses from across the centuries gives the resultant picture an authenticity often lacking in parallel discussions. Her argument, however, does not undermine our thesis. Whilst there are resonances in the tradition to which she can point, in certain aspects her argument feels indisputably modern. It need not clash with the arguments of Lampe and others, but rather enrich them and take them on a stage further. It does not alter the sense of the doctrine of the Trinity having changed over the Christian centuries, indeed having evolved from no argued doctrine at all in the New Testament. Furthermore, it is difficult to assess whether her resultant doctrine can be compared in any formal way with the traditional *essential* doctrine of the Trinity as confirmed at Chalcedon. This is no criticism of her argument, which is lucid and persuasive. It is, however, to suggest that the Trinity when revisited in this present age looks very different from its forbears of earlier times. Essential Trinitarianism in the sense meant by the early Church Fathers may now be an irrecoverable concept.

Development or Evolution?

Whilst this whirlwind tour of selected landscapes in the history of Trinitarian doctrine is unavoidably limited in its scope, it gives us sufficient snapshots to make clear the force of our argument. There is no inevitability about doctrinal growth and thus development as it has come to be understood is an inadequate concept. Historical analysis makes it clear that doctrine does not develop in the manner of a flower unfolding, or a seed bursting forth. Instead, the organism seems to produce unexpected 'sports' as new centuries open up before us. Hence it will survive only when it is fitted to its cultural, intellectual and spiritual context.

The process that we have just been describing, then, is very different from that set out by Newman in his *Essay*. The above reflections would have been implausible, however, without Newman's courageous affirmation of development in Christian doctrine. Even so, what we have described is not a process rooted in inevitability. Instead the evidence suggests that the process is far more complex. Using the biological model of evolution, a great variety of possibilities presented themselves in Patristic times and the ultimate embracing of a particular set of 'mutations' occurred through a process of selection. This process, then, implies a model of evolution analogous to that used in the biological sciences. How can we distinguish the positive and negative analogies implied? As in biology, so in theology – there must be a template or a substrate out of which any mutation arises. This will give us clues which enable us to identify parent and mutation as part of the same family. Then there is the process of mutation itself. Again, as in biology a variety of mutations will occur, but not all will survive. Finally, there is the process of selection. For the mutation to survive it must be 'fitted' to its environment. In the case of doctrine that means it must be capable of transmitting the family characteristics of Christian life and faith but mutated such that they can live in the prevailing cultural conditions.

Wherein lie the negative analogies? To begin with there is the question of continued invariance. In biology, the evidence shows the process of replication to be immensely conservative. Mutations are very rare indeed and would be inconsequential were it not for the vast number of replications happening in the course of each microsecond within the existence of a living organism. It is difficult to make an exact comparison at this point with theology. Biologically, different evolved species stand alongside each other at the same point in time. The only obvious parallel here lies in the doctrinal variety exemplified within different churches and different theological schools. On a fairly restricted level one can see this in viewing the Protestant Reformation. The doctrinal changes represented in the sixteenth century Reformation were clearly more 'fitted' to some environments than others. Even a cursory glance at the Lutheran phenomenon bears out this point. Within Germany itself the effects of the Reformation were patchy and some of this inheritance remains to this present day. Parts of Germany remained loyal to traditional catholicism, whereas other parts became reformed; north Germany remains far more Protestant than the south. The reasons for this uneven response to Luther were cultural, political, and even in some cases virtually accidental. Indeed, it is interesting to note that some of the issues that led to the divisions of the Church at that time no longer profoundly divide Protestant and Catholic. Different conditions prevail and some mutations now find themselves growing healthily in Protestant and Catholic circles alike. Attitudes to scripture and understandings of the liturgy are cases in point. The more crucial developments, however, are those which happen in the linear course of history although, as we shall see, there are divergences synchronically. Put crudely the question is: are there some elements of Christian faith which have mutated, while a vast residual element of the faith remains invariant? This question is impossible to answer with any accuracy since we cannot view the phenomenon longitudinally and objectively through history. 'The past is another country, they do things differently there' – we cannot recapture the consciousness of earlier ages in a manner which excludes all contingency and relativities.

A second negative analogy relates to the nature of the selection process. In biology there is a denial of any sense of purpose in the process, except in as much as that which survives is that which is best fitted to its environment. A particular mutation may have a teleonomic aspect to it, that is it may fulfill a project. Nevertheless its existence is quite accidental or fortuitous. The accidental nature of selection is modified in the theological model. Circumstances themselves, of course, may be random or adventitious; God allows humanity freedom to make its own mistakes. Alongside doctrinal questions can be ranged a number of cultural and political factors. How significant for cultural stability was the continuation of the pagan cult?[27] Was it politically expedient for the Emperor at certain points in history to defend the earlier paganism at the expense of

Christianity? How far had other religious influences moulded and shaped the growing body of Christian belief? Thus the facts relating to the life and death of Constantine, the battles that were fought and the politics that reigned, are all contingent; they could have happened otherwise, and we should not see them as divinely foreordained. This certainly means that very significant, influential, and indeed determinative elements in the formation of mutations (that is in the adaption of Christian doctrine) are contingent upon the vagaries of individual or corporate human behaviour. Despite these determinative elements, however, human freedom also plays an essential part in the selection process. If there are choices, human beings may decide. If there are different doctrinal formulations on offer, then the Christian community, by the grace of God, has the opportunity to discern which is the appropriate mutation. Decisions will be made to adapt the expression of Christianity to the culture in which it finds itself living.

In the case of the Council of Nicaea, it became clear that, for a variety of reasons, the Athanasian solution should be adopted. The precise point which an evolutionary view of doctrinal change makes is that the result was not predetermined, it was not inevitable. We should stress at this point that we are making no value-judgement about the process of doctrinal evolution. This is not a covert means of implying a form of cultural superiority for our age. Rather, it is seeing the evolution of doctrine as a means of describing what has actually happened. This in itself has important implications. As with biology, that which survives is that which is 'fitted' to the ecological circumstances and environment. So, we may feel it a pity that pterodactyls and mammoths no longer roam the earth, but the harsh fact is that they proved themselves unfitted for survival. So too with doctrine. To return to our earlier imagery, to revisit an earlier belief is often to discover a quite different expression of doctrinal concerns and their resolutions. Our perception of the problem is different, and indeed on occasions the landscape itself has changed. The world is now, at least to some extent, a different place; its challenges will also have changed, and fresh intellectual and social issues will press upon us.

The result of seeing doctrinal change in this light implies quite different means of assessing the process of adaptation within Christian belief, and thus also it will have further implications for our understanding of continuing Christian identity. It may help to revert to nineteenth century controversies for a moment. When opposing the newly propounded theory of evolution, Samuel Wilberforce's failure lay in being blind to Darwin's discovery. Darwin's theory said not that we are related to apes, as if they were close cousins, albeit three times removed. Instead, the challenge was that despite the radical differences between humanity and the apes, at some point in the process of evolution, from similar genetic roots, sprang and survived two quite distinct inheritors. The truth of this insight transferred to the theological canvas demands a reorientation for which 'development', as conceived by Newman, is an inadequate term. Doctrines may evolve in a number of ways, and cultural and historical factors could mean that two or more families of doctrine which now seem very different trace their origins to one common root. The Christianity of the Ethiopian Orthodox Church and that of Swiss Calvinism are worlds apart. Vincent Donovan's fascinating reflections on Christian mission in Africa illustrate this vividly. The implication of his thesis for Christian mission is that all one can do is to tell something of the Christian story and then wait for a response from within that culture. At one point he notes: 'The final missionary step as regards the people of any nation or culture, and the most important lesson we will ever teach them – is to leave them.'[28] Their response to the gospel story may be in the form of an evolutionary leap that had never been expected – will we recognise the gospel as it emerges from this new environment, and how can we be sure it has any authentic continuity with what has come to be known as orthodox Christianity? Will the landscape now have changed so radically as to appear unrecognisable and alien on any attempt to revisit?

It is questions like this that are raised by using the model of evolution for doctrinal change and adaptation. They are not new questions. The preferred model of evolution is not normative; it does not presume that a mutation is a rogue development within the Christian tradition. Any specific adaptation must be reviewed and criticised in the light of the wider tradition and also in the light of contemporary understanding. The model of evolution suggests that the process of doctrinal change may be even more complex than had hitherto been assumed. It suggests that the process of evolution is a corporate, relational, and to a certain extent random and unpredictable process, in the sense that it is at least partially at the mercy of human and thus historical vicissitudes.

A further way of looking at this, arising out of such an evolutionary perspective, is to think in terms of ecology and to imagine the history of doctrine (together with the wider history of Christian life and witness of which it is a part) as a dynamic, developing, evolving eco-system of interconnected doctrines, texts, practices and attitudes. As even primary school children are now learning, an eco-system is something that cannot be understood in terms of causality in the mechanistic sense, as if the whole system could be ultimately explained by being traced back through a chain of causes to a single primary cause. Such a system rather involves the interdependence of all the parts so that, for example, the hunter is dependent on the prey which in turn is dependent on its own food sources, etc. This is a very different way of looking at things from the nineteenth century view that would see the hunter, the predator, as the dominant figure, 'the winner' as it were, in the evolutionary drama of nature red in tooth and claw. In a similar way the evolutionary process of doctrine presents us with a vast and complex network of interacting elements. There is not necessarily a single line of development along which the history of doctrine, still less of the Church, has moved and in terms of which all theologies, liturgies and spiritualities can be evaluated. In other words, we cannot just assume that, for example, Roman Catholicism is the mainstream from which the Protestant and Orthodox Churches have separated or diverged – or, conversely, that Protestantism preserves the essence of the Gospel over against the corruptions and compromises of Rome. Liberal theology is not necessarily an 'advance' on traditionalism, whilst traditionalism or fundamentalism are not necessarily as ancient or as changeless as their advocates maintain.

Within the parameters of such rich and many-faceted interdependence, evolution continues still, without it the atmosphere spells death for Christianity, but equally our faith must always bear a clear resemblance to that which we believe to be at the heart of the gospel as seen in Jesus.

The Evolution of Doctrine

To revisit doctrine, then, is a complex and bewildering experience, as bewildering as our returns to childhood places and experiences. The landscapes will have changed, sometimes radically. Our perceptions will be different from those of earlier ages; doctrines, as we have seen, undergo reformulation and change. If that change is to be seen within a Christian context, then some means of establishing the process by which doctrine has been formed is essential. What were they trying to say, those who testified to essential Trinitarianism? Can their concerns be ours, and indeed can they be recovered? Are some of these issues lost beyond the mists of time, or has the doctrinal landscape changed such that earlier edifices have been razed to the ground? My adult return to my childhood seaside paradise was a salutary experience. It was painful and disappointing, but it was also cathartic and refreshing. Littlehampton ceased to be an idealised picture residing only in my dreams. I can be realistic about what to expect when next I revisit. The landscape has been remade anew, and beyond the disappointment lies a living vision which is a stimulus for future experience in seaside exploits.

Christian life issues out of an inheritance, lives in the present, but unerringly must look to the future in God. Landscapes will change and it is vital that as a community we understand the mechanism of that change if future vision is not to be usurped by past ideals or overtaken by an obsession with novelty. That is the nature of a Spirit-filled tradition. Accepting this truth, should we rather see doctrine as evolving? If this model does prove to be useful then it is bound to have significant implications for Christian identity.

How in the light of a theory of doctrinal evolution should we be able to decide what was an authentic evolutionary change? These questions require us to understand how we believe Spirit and tradition relate. They require of us too a response to questions about the interpretation of Holy Scripture. Is Scripture part of the means by which we identify the Christian community in succeeding ages, and indeed through which we view the evolution of doctrine?

As we explore these questions further it will become clear that the concept of communication is an especially valuable tool in formulating answers that do justice to the issues involved. In saying this we recognise not only that Spirit, tradition and Word each have an obvious concern with communication, but also that communication is a key provided specifically by evolutionary theory, since the communication of hereditary characteristics as of environmentally stimulated adaptions lies at the heart of any evolution. How then does the Christian gospel communicate itself?

Chapter 3

Spirit, Tradition and Change

The Great Funeral Procession

If it is the case that the Church is truly engaged in a process of evolutionary development then it has to be said that it doesn't always look like it! For many people – insiders and outsiders alike – it is of the essence of the Church that it doesn't change. Many – for good or ill – must have had the experience when taking part in some Church event (liturgical or social) of stepping back in time or of entering a world in which time stands still. Moreover, when change is mooted it seems invariably to occasion a level of anxiety and even trauma that is scarcely paralleled in the wider world. The Church clings – or is easily portrayed as clinging – to its institutions, forms and traditions with a degree of rigidity that verges on desperation. Nor is such a view confined to those critics who attack the Church from the outside. A number of years ago I heard a sermon by a preacher who had a reputation as one of the most 'successful' contemporary Pentecostal preachers in Latin America. His ministry had brought about the conversion of thousands amongst the shanty-towns of that region – that is, amongst people living in the most marginal of situations, lacking housing, good sanitation, medical care and the hope of economic betterment. They were people exposed also to the double violence of crime and of authorities whose scant respect for human rights is notorious. What would be his words to us, a comfortable English congregation which, though meeting in an inner city Church, could scarcely claim to have wrestled with problems of such magnitude? Some were expecting a blistering attack on the wealth of the West, on our indifference to the human suffering of the poor. Others, perhaps, expected to end the evening talking in tongues. Others were just interested.

43

In the event, the image which dominated his address was that of a funeral in which the coffin was followed by a long procession of mourners. The Church, he said, was all too often like that funeral procession, mourners lamenting a dead God and only capable, at best, of preserving his memory amongst them. Only where the Church was animated by the living presence of the Spirit, only where the Church existed in the present and out of its present experience of the Spirit could it be called 'alive'. Otherwise it was no more than a backward-looking cult of the dead, its traditions serving only to mummify the now lifeless belief that had once overturned empires and conquered the world. That, then, was how a Christian from one of the world's newest and most rapidly growing churches looked on us, representatives of this ancient, established form of 'Christendom'. It was not our lack of social concern he castigated, but our lack of religious vitality.

A similar understanding of the relationship between the Church and revelation was given near-classic expression in one of the most influential works of twentieth century theology, Karl Barth's Commentary on the Letter to the Romans. Writing in the shadow of the First World War, at a time when certainties were being called into question on all sides, Barth used the image of a 'dry canal' to explain the significance of 'the Law' for revelation and, in particular, the situations of those 'inside' the Law (the Jews) and of those 'outside' (the Gentiles) as explained in chapter two of Paul's Letter. Barth's dramatic words are worth quoting at length, since they give forceful expression to the view of Tradition that we are now exploring.

> The law is the revelation once given by God, given in its completeness. The law is the impression of divine revelation left behind in time, in history, in the lives of men; it is ... a dry canal which in a past generation and under different conditions had been filled with the living water of faith and of clear perceptions ... The men who *have the law* are the men who inhabit this empty canal ... they possess the form of traditional and inherited religion, or even the form of an experience which had once been theirs ... But revelation is from God; it cannot be compelled to flow between the banks of an empty canal. It can flow there; but it also fashions for itself a new bed in which to run its course, for

it is not bound to the impress which it once has made, but is free.[1]

Barth is, of course, here interpreting Paul on the relationship between Jew and Gentile, a relationship in which 'the Law', 'the dry canal', assumed a very specific shape around such issues as circumcision and dietary laws. Nonetheless it is clear from this passage – and spelt out elsewhere in his commentary – that everything which is said of the Jewish Law is potentially applicable to the contemporary Church, its institutions, its theology, its ethics. It too is nothing but a dry canal through which the water once flowed and may flow again – but is under no compulsion or necessity so to do.

This view of the Church is one which is now widespread – within the 'household of faith' as well as without. It is a view that sees the Church as subject to a familiar law of human affairs – '*Tout commence en mystique et finit en politique*' ('Everything begins in mysticism and ends with politics'). Original enthusiasm gives way to calculations of political self-interest and institutional survival. Such a view (we might call it a historical myth) is by no means limited to charismatics (as the example of Karl Barth shows!). It can even be found amongst theological liberals and radicals normally far removed from the charismatic wing of the Church in their theology. Here, for example, is the feminist version. According to this, the very earliest Church, under the immediate inspiration of Jesus's teaching and practice, broke through the assumed gender roles of both Jewish and Hellenistic culture, pioneering a community in which charismata, leadership and even apostolic authority could be held by women as well as by men. Gradually, however, after the initial period of expansion, the Church became organised in an authoritarian, patriarchal fashion. Indeed, the self-definition of 'The Church' over against a succession of heresies in the second century and later was in part prompted by the male leadership's desire to curb and limit the role played by women.

Similarly, a Marxist reading of Church history might extol the egalitarian aspects of the early community (as reflected, for example, in the holding of all goods in common), whilst bewailing the subsequent 'take-over' of the Church by an ecclesiastical hierarchy that both reflected and became identified with the hierarchy of the imperial state, a take-over reflected in the transformation of the poor man of Galilee into the Christ Pantokrator, the Cosmic Emperor enthroned above all creation, a figure familiar to us from Byzantine art. We might find comparable stories of decline and fall in, for example, pacifist circles or in the writings of a Kierkegaard or a Bonhoeffer, for whom the blood-witness, the witness who dies for the truth, is the pre-eminent model of discipleship.

Saying that these interpretations reflect a historical myth is not, of course, saying that they are insignificant or false. The process by which the Church became 'established' clearly involved transformations and redefinitions that are very plausibly read as compromise or sellout. What is being questioned here is the necessity, the inevitability, of seeing this process – as it is so often seen – in terms of a conflict between spirit and tradition. Even though Barth's image of 'the dry canal' allows for the possibility that the Spirit might again flow through the banks of the canal, there is, in his view, no intrinsic connection between the Spirit and the forms of tradition. It may flow again – it may not. It is a matter, even at best, of complete indifference. The assumption that there is a fundamental and categorical difference between Spirit and tradition is deeply rooted in the contemporary mind-set and interacts with a whole string of comparable oppositions: Spirit *vs* Letter, New *vs* Old (as in New Covenant *vs* Old Covenant), Gospel *vs* Law, Grace *vs* Works, Freedom *vs* Institution, Individual *vs* Society, Truth *vs* Vested Interest, – etc! etc! Such oppositions are plainly to be found in the New Testament itself. Jesus speaks of his message as the 'new wine' which will burst the 'old wineskins' and contrasts the 'commandment of God' with the 'tradition of men', whilst Paul defines his life as a Pharisee in terms of an over zealous following of the traditions of his ancestors (Gal. 1.14). Indeed, much of Paul's theology hinges on the deployment of such binary oppositions to define or to resolve the debates in which he engages with a succession of opponents. Karl

Barth's discussion of 'the empty canal' itself illustrates this by showing how Paul uses the duality of Spirit/revelation *vs* Law/tradition to break through the confrontation between Jew and Gentile in the Early Church.

'Any preacher knows', of course, that such distinctions are an invaluable (perhaps even an unavoidable) rhetorical tool. They serve to focus and clarify issues and choices. We might even speculate that the dominance of two-party systems in democratic societies witnesses to the very deep entrenchement of such habits of thought in human communities – and the comparably great difficulty in moving beyond them. Nonetheless (and such a move might come more easily to Anglicans than to some others) there comes a point at which it is necessary to recognise that such oppositions possess a both-and as well as an either-or character and that neither singly nor together do they finally determine the character of lived experience. Let us then see if we can find a more positive view of 'tradition', a view which does not exclude Spirit-experience (nothing, after all, can do that: the wind blows where it wills) but rather shows the positive possibilities for a dovetailing of Spirit-and-Tradition. In pursuing such a view we shall also be exploring how those factors working for innovation in the life of the Church *and* those that serve the cause of continuity share a common root in the essential dynamics of Christian communication.

Tradition: A New Testament View

If we read Paul's admonitory words to the Corinthians (1 Cor. 11.17–34) regarding the keeping of the Lord's supper we shall not find the word 'tradition' (Gk: *paradosis*) as such. Nevertheless, this passage throws much light on what is essentially involved in the process of tradition – particularly if we read it in the light of what we know of Paul's own conversion and related spiritual experiences. Having torn his readers off a strip for the selfish and disorderly manner in which they keep the Lord's supper, Paul recalls them to the basics of what it is all about in words which still stand at the heart of most Eucharistic rites (vv. 23–25). What is of particular interest for our present discussion are the words

'For I received from the Lord what I also passed on [AV:delivered] to you.' There are two points here we need to notice. The first is Paul's claim that what he is about to tell the Corinthians is something he received 'from the Lord'; the second is the model of receiving-and-delivering around which the text turns. Let us look at these in more detail.

Commentators are both intrigued and at variance with one another about the precise meaning of the claim that what Paul received regarding the words of institution he received 'from the Lord'. Clearly, two possibilities present themselves. The first is that these specific words were somehow communicated to Paul in the mode of an ecstatic spiritual experience. Such a claim would fit with the character of Paul's apostleship as an apostleship established directly by Christ himself without the mediation of apostolic fellowship. In this respect it might be contrasted with the apostleship of Peter and the others which was rooted in (even if not ultimately validated by) their having shared the human companionship of Jesus 'according to the flesh'. Paul's 'call', on the other hand, came in a completely individual manner, its only pre-history being (in Paul's mind, at least) in the mysterious providence of the God who had already separated him for this work from the time when he was in his mother's womb. Paul himself claims that in the wake of his Damascus-Road conversion and calling 'I did not consult with any man, nor did I go up to Jerusalem to see those who were apostles before I was ...' (Gal. 1.16–17). Whether or not we identify the experience described in 2 Corinthians 12 with that initial conversion experience and whether or not Paul is using the phrase 'I know a man in Christ ...' to refer indirectly to himself, his account of how the visionary is caught up into 'the third heaven' (or even 'paradise') does seem to imply the belief that such ecstatic experience could yield knowledge of spiritual realities. Similarly, the account of Paul's conversion in Acts seems to hinge on the possibility of actual verbal communication taking place between the heavenly and the earthly worlds. Clearly, then, we cannot rule out the possibility that Paul might have had – in either the conversion or 'third heaven' experiences or at some other time – specific revelations regarding the Lord's supper, thus receiving them 'from the Lord'.

The other possibility is that, despite Paul's disclaimer regarding his having conferred with 'flesh and blood', he did undergo some kind of catachesis after conversion. Such a possibility might be hinted at in the account in Acts when, after his baptism by Ananias, we are told that Paul (still Saul at this point) spent 'several days with the disciples in Damascus' (Acts 9.19). Is this an allusion to a period of post-baptismal instruction? Or, on similar lines, we might take the view that his fifteen-day conference, three years later, with Peter in Jerusalem (Gal. 1.18) involved the passing on of certain key traditions, amongst them the tradition regarding the Lord's supper.

Perhaps we shall never know the exact sense of these words, 'received from the Lord', in the sense of being able to reconstruct the history that lay behind them. Yet whichever line of interpretation appeals to us most what is clear is that, for Paul, the words (together, of course, with the practices they recommend) have full authority 'from the Lord'. Indeed, isn't the point precisely this: that our line of questioning presupposes a division which didn't exist for Paul himself, a division, that is, between experience on the one hand and instruction on the other, between 'Spirit' and 'tradition'. The point of qualifying the words by saying that they are 'from the Lord' is that they have, for Paul, and are to have, for his readers, the immediacy, the urgency and the force of present experience. To see in more detail what this involves let us move on to examine the model of 'receiving-and-delivering' that informs our text.

Like the Latin-based 'tradition' (= 'trans' [across] + 'do' [give]) by which it is usually translated, the Greek term *para-dosis* essentially means 'giving over', 'handing across', 'giving up' and even 'surrendering'. Although it is relatively rare as a noun in the New Testament (occurring mostly in the negative sense of those human 'traditions' that stand in the way of the gospel) its verbal form is more common. (This itself is already an important clue to what needs to be said in any contemporary theory of tradition, and it is a point to which we shall return.) Interestingly there are two quite distinct uses of this verbal form in the passage at which we are now looking. This first is when Paul speaks of his 'passing on' or 'delivering' to the Corinthians the word which he 'received from the Lord'. The second comes when he speaks of 'the night [Jesus] was *betrayed*', 'betrayed' here developing the sense of 'delivering over' as a physical, bodily act, as in handing over a prisoner to an enemy. It is a sense used, dramatically, by Jesus when, in Gethsemane, he declares, 'Look, the hour is near, and the Son of man is betrayed into the hands of sinners.' (Matt. 26.45)

These two very different connotations give an extraordinary depth to these lines.

First of all they set up a contrast between that kind of 'handing over' which is the work of faith – the faithful delivery of that with which we have been entrusted by God – and that kind of 'handing over' which is the work of sin – the faithless 'giving over' of the living word of God 'into the hands of sinners': in the presence of Jesus the Lord, in the coming of the Word of God 'in the flesh' human beings are given responsibility for accepting or rejecting that Word and for determining their own destiny by the nature of their response. The readers of Paul's Letter are, in effect, being asked 'Which kind of "handing over" are *you* going to be party to?' To modern readers, used to living with a high level of moral and intellectual freedom (at least, superficially) such a statement might seem unremarkable: but the New Testament is declared in a context in which Truth is understood as something 'given', something within which we have to live – not something over which we have power. That is part of *its* disturbing power, that it neutralises the power of the 'traditions of the ancestors' in favour of what we would now call 'subjective decision'. In virtually every sentence the New Testament is a text about choice, about the 'two ways' that confront us at every juncture of our lives.

Secondly (and implicit within everything that has just been said), the juxtaposition of these two meanings reminds us that the basic physicality of the act of handing over is strikingly relevant in a context which concerns the way in which the Lord's supper is to be kept. For this supper – whatever else it may also be – is a literal handing over of physical, material things. The way in which the participants reverence each other by recognizing and responding to each other's basic needs regarding food and drink is central to the meaning of the total act. It takes shape in that dimension of our lives in which *by virtue of our embodiment* we are continually and utterly dependent on one another. Angels might not be so interdependent. Human beings are. Moreover, there is a complete analogy between the way in which we assume or repudiate responsibility for this interdependence and the way in which we receive or reject the embodied Word. Reflect, for a moment, on the act of trust made by anyone undergoing an operation involving general anaesthesia. Such a person (or their relatives) completely 'hands over' their body to the care of others, putting their life in the hands of others. So, the question of tradition, as that is raised by our text, goes something like this: Do we 'hand over' the Word as we would handle the body of a loved one whose life was in our hands – or do we 'hand it over' as Christ was handed over to be abused, tortured and put to death? Will the supper be kept not merely as a symbol but as an event of reverence and love – or will it be an occasion of violence and division (as, Paul fears, it has almost become amongst the Corinthians)?

It is worth recalling that in the passage we are studying 'tradition' does not occur as a noun, but as a verb – 'a doing word'. 'Tradition' is not a static 'deposit of faith' that simply gets passed, unchanged, from hand to hand. 'Tradition' as verb is the active process of transmission, the receiving and giving of spiritual reality. It is – to recall Barth – not 'the dry canal' but the flowing water, the water that brings, that is, life. Remembering that the whole context of this discussion is the Lord's supper, the central sacramental act at the heart of the Church's worshipping life, we might say that there is no knowledge in the New Testament of ritual or liturgy that has come to stand like a dead letter over against the enthusiasm of a living worshipping community. The tradition is not a set of fixed words, a formula, accompanying the handing over of the elements of bread and wine; the tradition is, on the contrary, the whole event of a faithful handing over of the life of Christ's body. The Lord's supper itself – though with no reference to later theories such as transubstantiation – is 'the tradition' and, as such, a real communication of the living reality of Christ, a real means of union between Christ and the believer, a real presence of his saving acts and forgiving grace.

'Tradition', as the faithful handing over of the Lord's word concerning the symbolic enactment of his presence in the community is not simply a 'means' of communication, 'delivering' a content which is ultimately indifferent to the form it is given. It is itself that which it communicates – or, to put it another way, it is what it is by virtue of what it has to communicate. 'The medium is the message'. To a certain extent it is in this respect like a good work of art: good art is never simply a visual aid providing a short cut to an idea or a truth which we could, in principle, come to know by some other (if more laborious) route. Good art simply communicates itself. Rembrandt's self-portraits (to take an example more or less at random) are not 'explained' by their place in art history, by the economic forces of early capitalism, or by what was going on in the mind of the artist as he painted them. If 'explanation' is relevant at all, then they 'explain' themselves. The painting itself is what we need to see – and nothing else – when we look at these (or any other) great pictures. We get 'more' by looking at the picture than we do from the explanation!

It is also worth noticing that the communication process, which tradition is, is essentially contagious: 'As my father has sent me, I am sending you'; 'I received from the Lord what I also passed on to you …' It is a process the very essence of which is communication and as such infinitely open-ended: each real, effective act of communication generates further acts of communication; what I have received I must pass on, if I am not to falsify the very fact of my having received it in the first place; I have only really received if I am also giving out. Communication constantly overflows itself; in doing so it both generates and *is* the life of the community. It is easy to see from this that it is also always developing or, to use a notion we have already explored at some length, evolving.

Recalling the emphasis on the present, almost bodily nature of tradition in Word and sacrament it need scarcely be added that this whole process is not about the communication of some intellectual 'idea' but about the very real communication of human mutuality: in a word, it is the communication of love (in both senses of the word 'of': love is both the content and the means of the communication). The community in which Word, Spirit and sacrament are real is also – and cannot be anything but – a community of love, of mutual openness, acceptance and affirmation, a community that knows 'peace' in the full prophetic sense. Yet it should also be emphasised that the love and the peace which in this way characterise the communicating community are real only as they are themselves 'received' and then 'delivered' on. They are real for us as members of that community only as we allow ourselves to be part of the flow of communication. There is no island, no stronghold in which we could hide them away for our own enjoyment as if they were individual possessions, 'things' we 'have'. At each moment the choice (which was previously noted as a constant accompaniment of evangelical communication) remains real: the choice to believe or to be offended, the choice to allow the process to go on, in and through us – or to opt out and try to take as possession what can only be lived as communion.

These comments also reflect the wider sense of Paul's words to the Corinthians. In warning them that they cannot have a proper celebration of the Lord's supper if each individual or clique is self-centredly satisfying its own needs before giving whatever energy and attention is left to the community, he is, at one level, simply spelling out the implications of what is involved in authentic communication, in 'tradition', understood as the making present of the Lord in the midst of his community. It is no coincidence that Paul's discussion of the tradition of the Lord's supper leads on to a consideration of spiritual gifts that culminates in the famous eulogy of love in chapter thirteen of the Letter. This chapter completes the sense of tradition as the Church, in and by means of the Lord's supper, communicating itself to itself as love. It also points to a wider sense of tradition, the tradition of active discipleship, since such love cannot be limited to the time and the place of a weekly gathering: love is a personal quality, a personal activity, that gives shape to a whole life.

Tradition, in this wider sense, becomes the tradition of a 'way' of being and living in the world. It is, so to speak, the communication of the Christian 'style' that informs and is manifest in every aspect of Christian living.

Word and Spirit

If 'tradition' can be understood as central to the 'making present' of spiritual reality, then we can begin to see how there is a profound congruence between tradition, Word and Spirit – not to mention, of course, the sacramental action of the Lord's supper as the specific form of the tradition we have been examining.

A similar understanding of tradition and sacrament (although focused, this time, on baptism) is to be found in the writings of the nineteenth century theologian, poet and educationalist, N. F. S. Grundtvig[2]. Little known outside his native Denmark, Grundtvig is there hailed as 'Denmark's greatest son', a man whose vision of the People's High Schools transformed the educational life of Denmark and at the same time enabled the Danish Lutheran Church to provide a continuing spiritual focus for those outside the nation's educated élite. It is impossible to summarise Grundtvig's wide-ranging work, which combined the redis-covery of Denmark's Nordic inheritance with a vision of Christianity that was at once evangelical and fervently national. At the same time, this vision provided an alterna-tive to the rationalising theology of those who sought to 'update' Christianity along the lines laid down by contempo-rary intellectual thought and yet was still sufficiently human to appeal to those who were not of a sectarian or revivalist disposition. (One of Grundtvig's rallying-calls was 'First a human being, and then a Christian', meaning that Christianity would only truly flourish when the believer was also fully-developed emotionally, socially and intellectually.)

What Grundtvig himself called his 'incomparable dis-covery' was the theory of 'the living Word', a theory which he developed in response to the attacks on the Bible being mounted by rationalist critics. What Grundtvig came to realise was that if Christianity makes itself dependent on the written letter of scripture, then it is going to be all too vulnerable to such attacks. In any case, such over-reliance on the written word makes the ordinary believer dependent on, for example, the translator and, more generally, on the whole company of learnèd scribes and commentators, who may themselves be orthodox – but, then again, may not! 'So long as we try to derive the faith from scripture,' Grundtvig wrote, 'we shall be arguing till the Day of Judgement with our enemies about what the Christian faith is that we are to defend; so long also will the Christian community remain in uncertainty, vexed by all those innumerable doubts which arise when one is reading an ancient book which has gone through many hands and which has so many-sided, so profound, and therefore often necessarily so obscure a content as the Bible has.'[3] Instead of trying to *base* the faith on the Bible, Grundtvig looked instead to what he called 'the living word', that is, the confession of faith spoken at baptism by the believer. There are obvious problems in identifying the Apostle's Creed as we now know it with that 'living word', as Grundtvig tried to do, problems which concern both the historical basis for such an identification and the charge that Grundtvig is herewith reducing the essence of Christianity to the mere repetition of a set of words learnt by rote. Yet there is much to commend Grundtvig's instinct for rooting the continuity of the Church in its continuing sacramental life. For it is precisely in the sacramental life of the Church that that process of receiving-and-delivering that we have called 'tradition' lives, a process made concrete in the spoken affirmations that are a necessary condition of participating in it. The words of the actors are the words of acceptance, of affirmation, of proclamation that both bind them to the tradition and that make the tradition live (indeed if no one ever said them, the tradition – and with it the Church – would soon come to an end). They are the words that make this process happen and that, by so doing, also ensure that those who speak them take responsibility for it, for they are words spoken in the first person: 'I [We] believe ...' They are words that make the tradition something that belongs to and is carried forward by these particular individuals and not some impersonal force.

Our habits of mind might lead us to distinguish sharply between the tangible reality of the material elements used in sacraments, a reality that sustains the analogy between the embodied life of Jesus and the physical presence of the community in its acts of assembly, and the more refined, intellectual character of 'the Word'. But Grundtvig's idea of 'the Living Word' goes some way towards showing how Word and Sacrament are interdependent.

We might also explore this interdependence by other means, by, for example, a further consideration of the 'embodied' character of the communication process that is tradition. This bodily character of evangelical communication is not confined to sacramental acts. Most obviously, Paul's letters are themselves physical objects which need to be handed over manually, just as a postman today physically delivers his letters. More importantly, however, the ancient world had a far more concrete view of language than that which we perhaps presuppose today. How often the Old Testament prophets spoke of their 'Word' from the Lord as something that had an almost physical, almost independent existence – an understanding vividly symbolised when Ezekiel is ordered to eat a scroll containing the words of the Lord which he is to speak to the people of Israel (Ezek. 2.9–3.3). Such an understanding can also be sensed in the Johannine writings in which the bodily, incarnate reality of 'the Word' is stressed again and again: 'the Word' is not just something written, read, spoken, heard – it is something to be seen with the eyes and to be touched and handled (1 John 1.1–2). Similarly, for Paul, the Word which he has been given to proclaim is not simply a message 'about' Christ; it is rather a Word in which Christ himself is present, a Word which brings about and makes present the forgiveness, the reconciliation, the peace which it declares. Even so, as has just been suggested, this Word, in its physical, tangible, present reality, does not seek to compel the response of the receiver; there is always the possibility that the receiver's response might be 'No' rather than 'Yes' (in the same way that even those who were confronted with the bodily presence of Jesus could opt to 'deliver' him 'over' into the 'hands of sinners').

But if we are now assimilating the Word to sacrament and to tradition, what about the relationship between Word and Spirit?

It is important at this point not to confuse the Pauline categories. For Paul there may well be an opposition between 'Letter' (*gamma*) and 'Spirit'. This is an opposition which comes into being when the Word is written down, codified, legalised and transformed into a quasi-objective power, detached from the context of living speech, when, in fact, it becomes 'Law'. But there is no hint of any fundamental conflict between 'Spirit' and 'Word'. On the contrary 'Spirit' and 'Word' alike are powers that enable the actualisation of the gospel, that enable the good news of salvation to become real and to become powerful in the lives of the recipients of the message. They are alike modes of the divine working within the created order. As such they are both media of divinity and fully concrete, fully actual forms of presence.

Perhaps the most powerful expression of the congruence between Word and Spirit is to be found in John's gospel, in the scene in which the resurrected Lord appears amongst his disciples and breathes on them the Holy Spirit – a scene sometimes described as the Johannine Pentecost (see John 20.19–23). This event narrates four principle empowerments. Firstly, it is a bestowing of peace, secondly, it is for mission ('as my Father has sent me, I am sending you'); thirdly, it gives the reality of the Spirit and fourthly it confers authority to offer forgiveness of sins. The narration emphasises throughout the interdependence of Word and Spirit: what the Lord promises in his Word, he also gives, here and now; also, it is suffused by a sense of the bodily nature of this communication: it is not, as we might put it, merely verbal, but an actual communication of energy, the transmission of life-force from one being to others. He *is* the Word. The Spirit *is* his Spirit.

We previously cited Bishop Grundtvig in the context of linking the communication processes of Word and Tradition. It might now be added that he is, in the words of E. L. Allen, 'pre-eminently the poet of Whitsuntide and the Holy Spirit'.[4] Although, as Denmark's most prolific hymn-writer, Grundtvig's hymns cover the whole compass of the liturgical year, his hymns for Pentecost are particularly significant,

celebrating at one and the same time the rebirth of nature
in the Danish countryside and the spiritual rebirth both of
the individual believer and of the community of faith.
Amongst other themes he marks how the agency of the
Holy Spirit is active within human language, enabling it
to become a medium of the divine word. The Spirit is 'God's
voice on life's way, Heaven's power of speech' without which
we cannot confess Jesus as Lord; yet, if the community is to
be what it is called to be, then it must pray 'Spirit of God, be
our tongue and our utterance', the Spirit 'creates[s] the word
in our mouth which is [otherwise] only a letter' – and when
this happens 'the mouths of the people acquire speech, the
native tongue interprets the Spirit of God.'[5] Spirit, to use an
expression from contemporary philosophy, creates an 'ideal
speech situation', a situation, that is, in which words are
charges with fulness of meaning and make present, one to
another, those engaged in the communication process – in
this case 'the whole company of heaven'. Human language is
rendered divine; divine language, human.

What we have been aiming at throughout this discussion is
an understanding of Word, Spirit and Tradition as interdependent (and constantly interactive) concrete forms of communication that make present the reality of the evangelical
content of the communication – and, in the act of making-
present *are* that reality. For that reality is itself good communication, communication of presence, communication that is
love. Such a view has been beautifully summarised by Johann
Adam Möhler, a Catholic theologian writing in the 1820s:
'Tradition is the expression of that Holy Spirit who enlivens
the community of believers – an expression that courses
through all ages, living at every moment, but always finding
embodiment.'[6] In reflecting on these words we should again
remind ourselves that this does not concern merely what
happens in the context of specifically 'religious' or liturgical
occasions, but has to do with the whole quality and style of
Christian living.

Shaping Tradition

The understanding of tradition which this chapter is
concerned to explore (and to recommend!) may, on the basis

of what has been said so far, be accused of being essentially shapeless – a pure, content-free communication process, which is its own end and its own reward. But though it is true that tradition in the sense developed here is not anxious about finding external props with which to back up its claims and does not – cannot – regard its own content as something external to its own processes, this is not at all to say that it is without content, that it is not *specific*. On the contrary, its very concreteness, its growth and development out of very specific acts of personal communication – of, for example, Paul delivering to his Corinthian readers that which he had received 'from our Lord' – means that its life is at all times concrete, definite, specific. It is never a matter of merely nebulous aspirations after 'spirituality'. Though not easy to define, Christian spirituality, the Christian 'style', is always definite.

What is it, then, in the process of tradition that ensures such definition? We suggest that it is the fact that tradition comprises a process of active remembering, a process that sustains continuity in the midst of change even as at the same time it generates changes out of that which gives continuity. Thinking back to Karl Barth's contrast between the rigid forms of human tradition and the living flow of the Spirit, a contrast expressed in the image of the canal and the water that once flowed between its banks but now flows elsewhere, we might comment that, of course, water is not completely changeable: wherever it flows it is still water, its invisible molecular structure means that however varied its form it is also in vital respects continuous with itself. Given that we have sought to break down the sharpness of Barth's distinction in favour of a single process of Spirit-and-Tradition and would therefore allow tradition to have something of the living, flowing quality that he reserves for Spirit, we may say that within tradition, memory is something like the molecular structure that ensures continuity in the midst of change. This memory, in a sense, is what, in the context of the first Christian century, became the basis of scripture, the oral tradition out of which the written text was produced. But the memory of the Church does not end with the closing of the canon of scripture. As the process of tradition continues, so that memory is constantly being enriched and enlivened. Sometimes it is a memory that acquires form in the shape of a standard text or exemplary life – the *Confessions* of an Augustine or the story of an Elizabeth Fry, the *Book of Common Prayer* or the self-sacrifice of the martyrs. Sometimes it is a memory preserved – for the time being – amongst a small group of believers, perhaps only by one, whilst sometimes it is a memory that has faded to be refreshed only at the last day. It appears in innumerable forms – as innumerable as the life of the Church itself is manifold. In whatever forms it does appear, however, it provides for continuity and definiteness within the natural, spontaneous self-shaping of tradition, of the communication, the receiving-and-delivering of faith and of all that is involved in that.

In the positive evaluation of tradition we are making here, we find ourselves close to such Roman Catholic theologians as Yves Congar, whose thought was a major inspiration for Vatican II. Congar notes that Protestants have always been reluctant to allow any sense or value to tradition other than as a mere vehicle or form by which to carry through history the unchanging truth once delivered to the apostles. Acknowledging that it is the gospel and not the tradition that is the *source* of theology, Congar also emphasizes that tradition is not merely an external form or means of communication, but contributes to the content of what is communicated. 'The tradition received by each one of us,' he says

> is not the quintessence of primitive Christianity, but the totality of what has been revealed about Christ over long ages. Nothing that is of value in past acquisitions has been lost. In principle, at each moment, one could make a summing up of what has thus been received and lived. It is this summing up which 'positive theology' (in the strict sense) struggles to attain. It searches out, in the documents which have come down to us, the full catholic meaning of the deposit as it has been affirmed and unfolded through the whole community of faith springing from the apostles.[7]

'Tradition', he remarks elsewhere, 'is not the simple permanence of a structure, but a continual renewal and fertility *within* this given structure, which is guaranteed by a living and unchanging principle of identity.'[8] For Congar too it is out of the relationship between Christ and the Spirit that the element of continuity is to be understood. He thus understands the history of Spirit-and-Tradition as a continuation of the history sketched in Hebrews 11:

> It was by faith, fulfilling the Gospel and by a 'mission' of the Holy Spirit, that the Council of Nicaea ...; it was by faith ... that St. Augustine ...; by faith ... that Francis Xavier ...; Thérèse Martin, and so on. This history retails [sic] Christians' responses to the calls of God and of time; it is made up of councils, acts of the magisterium, missionary endeavours and religious foundations, of conversions and decisions taken for God; but also the more secret history, to be disclosed only at the last judgement, of all the movements of faith and love drawn from our human freedom by God's grace.[9]

Congar's reference to the role of the magisterium (the teaching authority of the Papacy) inevitably points to the notorious difficulty that not all Christians can yet agree as to what counts as an authentic part of the tradition. Yet, without minimizing the seriousness of such conflicts (which, after all, still lead in some regions of the world to the shedding of blood), need we deny the positive aspect of tradition as a continual enrichment of the content of faith *so long as we remember that it is, finally, only God who decides what truly belongs to authentic tradition, It is only God to whom the secrets of all hearts are open, but, on the basis of the revelation in Christ, our expectation and our journey must be in the Spirit of hope and we cannot accept our present divisions as final.*

Past, present and future perspectives are united in some of the most striking words on tradition, memory and the life of the Church which have ever been written. They come from the writings of Nicholas Berdyaev, a Russian thinker of the first half of the twentieth century.

'The life of the Church,' he declared,

> rests upon holy tradition and succession. It is through tradition that in each new generation man enters into the same spiritual world. Tradition is a supra-personal ... experience, the creative spiritual life transmitted from generation to generation, uniting the living and the dead and thereby overcoming death. Death reigns in the world indeed but is vanquished in the Church.

Tradition is the memory which brings resurrection, the victory over corruption, the affirmation of eternal life. The tradition of the Church is not an authority imposed from without. It is a real and intrinsic victory over the division created by time; it is a glimpse of eternity in the mortal flight of time, a union of past, present and future in the oneness of eternity.[10]

Elsewhere he writes:

Memory of the past is spiritual; it conquers historical time. This however is not a conserving, but a creatively transfiguring memory. It wishes to carry forward into eternal life not that which is dead in the past but what is alive, not that which is static in the past but what is dynamic. This spiritual memory reminds man, engulfed in his historical time that in the past there have been great creative movements of the spirit and that they ought to inherit eternity ... Society is always a society not only of the living but also of the dead; and this memory of the dead ... is by no means a conservatively static memory, it is a creative dynamic memory. The last word belongs not to death but to resurrection.[11]

These words tell us that the life of the Church is a life which, through the process of receiving-and-delivering embraces the urgency of the present while maintaining a dialogue with the past. It is a dialogue which, as anticipating the resurrection, also points toward that great final consummation when the 'whole company of heaven' whose presence we now invoke in worship behold one another in their beholding and adoring of God and see not only God but also each other face to face. Yet that process and that dialogue themselves arose, for Christians, out of resurrection, out of the receiving-and-delivering of that new hope, that new Word, that new Spirit, which was kindled amongst the apostles in the aftermath of their master's death.

We have come a long way from seeing the tradition of the Church in terms of a long and mournful funeral procession or of a barren and arid 'dry canal'. We are rather choosing to see tradition as the living water that sustains the Church in life and fills to overflowing the channelled banks of history. Yet it remains true that nothing that has been said can justify everything that passes for Church tradition. Within the order of time all human traditions sooner or later pass their sell-by date. But that is not the point. The point is that tradition

itself lives and points towards the resurrection of all goodness in the midst of the change and decay to which all flesh is
heir. Tradition is not a matter of timeless truths but a process
of spiritual exchange, of dynamic, vital love.

It has been said that the Church is whatever we say it is.
This bold statement draws attention to the way in which the
actual unfolding of the process of tradition shapes for each
generation and for each community what the Church is for
that time and for those people. What, for example, the local
Church is, the way it conducts its affairs (in and out of
'Church' in the narrow sense), the people who compose it,
the character of its worship and the style of its mission are
what will, for that time and place, determine what those
outside and those of the new generation experience as 'the
Church'. The ungodly business habits of a leading 'pillar of
the Church' will bring to life the charges of pharisaical
hypocrisy that are never far from people's minds in considering the Church, whilst the saintly sick-visiting of another
member of the community will play a counter-acting role. By
being delivered over to the process of tradition the Church as
it exists comes to bear an enormous responsibility. That
which we do, that which we say, that which we are as – and
in the way that – we receive-and-deliver the gospel entrusted
to us, the sacraments of redemption, the transfigured
memory of the past: all this is itself the raw material of future
transfiguration and future resurrection. There is no other
way through time than the way we actually tread. The saying
'The Church is whatever we say it is' might seem to be an
expression of pride, an example of human beings usurping
what belongs only to God. It is, however, better understood
as drawing attention to the humbling responsibility involved
in seeing the Church as tradition, tradition that itself
contains and nourishes the hope that, at the same time, the
Church is more than we are able to make it. For the tradition
is shaped by its memory and its memory both speaks for
confidence in the forgiveness of that in which we fall short
and in turn shapes the expectation that 'all shall be well' and
that 'the last word belongs not to death but to resurrection.'

Chapter 4

Re-reading the Bible

Memory and Interpretation

We have been thinking about the development of doctrine in
terms of the model of evolution, as bringing forth new forms
that could never have been simply 'deduced' from what was
there before not yet merely 'developing' in the way that the
bud develops into the blossom. We have thought about the
Church, under the rubrics of 'Spirit' and 'Tradition' as a
complex living process of change, constantly re-shaping and
re-forming itself in the course of its journey through history
and we have touched on how, in the midst of that process, it
cherishes a living memory of its own past. But there may well
be questions as to *how* the Church, here and now, remembers its past – and how it integrates the memory of that past
into its forward-moving engagement with the issues of the
present. And, although we have spoken to some extent about
'the Word' (especially as 'the living Word', the oral communication of faith to faith) we have so far said little about the
Word as scripture. Is scripture being understood as 'the letter
that kills'? And isn't it necessarily the case that in the scriptures – as in the doctrinal formulations of the universal councils – the content of orthodox Christianity is pre-determined
in such a way that the only real place for change is in the way
in which this pre-determined content is presented? To speak
the language of contemporary politics: isn't it a matter of
presentation, not of policy? Aren't the scriptures an *essential*
memory that the Church is obliged to pass on from generation to generation intact and unaltered? Here, it would seem
is something that doesn't – mustn't – change. How, then,
does scripture relate to the process of tradition that we have
described? What does the approach we are taking imply for

the interpretation of scripture? This question is one which theologians would describe as belonging to the discipline known as hermeneutics.

We shall return to this shortly, but let us begin by going back to the experience of re-visiting an old childhood haunt. When we thought about that experience before it was with an eye to the necessity of accepting where we are now, i.e., that the place we once knew has, in our absence, changed and there can be no going back. But what about my experience of myself in that past? How does the adult I am now relate to the child I was then? As I walk up the rather insignificant stone cutting my friends and I used to call 'The Bear's Cave' and which evoked all the terrors and challenge's of humanity's primeval past in our childish minds; as I look up at the twenty foot rock face which I then regarded as more or less the equivalent of Mount Everest (and myself as Sir Edmund Hillary); or, as I stroll along the beach where I made my first embarrassed attempts at teenage romance – how do I feel about all that?

It's easy to imagine a number of very different answers to that question. I might, for instance, be rather ashamed – if not in general then in certain particulars. If my own child were accompanying me on this trip down memory lane there might be certain things I would carefully avoid mentioning, knowing that to do so would be seriously to damage my credibility in his or her eyes! I might, on the other hand, sigh deeply and say to myself, 'If only it could always be like that. If only I could recapture that sense of newness and of wonder in which everything was then enveloped.' There might be memories which still angered or saddened me, events with which I still had not come to terms – or that whole epoch might be bathed in a uniform golden glow.

The process of re-evaluating our own past (or, as the case may be, of confirming the valuations we already made long ago) is, of course, not just something that happens when we go back after a long absence to some place we knew long ago – although it's particularly vivid in such contexts. It's a process we're engaged in all the time in normal social activity as we talk about ourselves, about the things we've done, the places we've been, the people we've met and so on. If we think about it for long we probably notice that, in fact, our relation to our own past is always changing, be it ever so slightly, an inch at a time. Each time we tell an anecdote we change it or change the way we tell it just a little bit; sometimes, as members of our family have doubtless noticed, the final version is almost unrecognisably transformed from the first fumbled telling! We may ourselves come to see, perhaps through the way in which others respond, that a story which we once thought showed us in a good light does no such thing and it may have to be dropped from our repertoire (or else, maybe, we henceforth tell it against ourselves). In such ways our relation to the past (here our own past) is one of *interpretation*: we never simply 'remember', but, in remembering, we also mostly quite spontaneously – interpret the past.

It is interesting how easily and how quickly we have slipped from the theme of remembering to the situation of people exchanging anecdotes and engaging in conversation. We all (or most of us) spend a very considerable part of our lives talking to one another. Talking and (to a much lesser extent, a cynic might add) listening come naturally to human beings. Even before we can talk 'properly' we babble away in baby talk and from then on the flow of language never stops. Even when we're on our own we carry on talking to ourselves, for thinking itself is usually accompanied by a flow of words – and that's as true for the least educated person as it is for the university professor. But, in the midst of this stream of words, we very rarely pause to reflect on the miracle of language, a miracle that's especially remarkable in the form of conversation. The conversation doesn't have to be about anything particularly profound or earth-shattering. Let it be a group of friends sitting around over coffee or in the pub or at a dinner party. Just reflect on the complexity of what's going on, think of the enormous number of sounds and combinations of sounds that go into ten minutes' worth of talk; then think about how each of those taking part 'translate' those sounds into words and sentences – a process doubly astonishing if, as very often happens, several members of the group have quite distinctive accents so that the sounds they utter are different from, but the words they speak are the same as those of the other talkers; next, those words are 'imagined' and 'understood' by the listeners, perhaps conjuring up in everybody's mind a more or less distinct picture of events they never themselves took part in, places they'd never themselves been (as when I was telling you about places from my childhood holidays); but, already, two or three people are talking back, the group makes a quick decision as to who is to have the word, and the original speaker is questioned or contradicted or clapped or applauded – and so it goes on ... So extraordinary is this most ordinary event that if we did try to think about it as it was happening we would be unable to cope. But again, note how the to and fro of words is not simply a mechanical process; we don't just hear or absorb or expectorate words. All the time we're speaking and listening we're *interpreting* trying to understand, trying to make sense.

These are just two examples of how interpretation is involved in everyday life and it would be easy to extend the list: watching a film, reading a book, learning a foreign language (just for fun, re-run the description of a normal conversation in the previous paragraph in a situation where all the others are native French speakers and you are doing your best to join in!), 'reading' the movements of the opposition's midfield, listening to an election address, thinking about the significance of crime statistics, going out for a romantic evening, etc., etc.

It is this question of interpretation that theologians are addressing when they speak of 'hermeneutics'. The word itself is off-putting, but at its simplest it just means 'the art of interpretation', that is, knowing about the ways and means we most of us already use in interpreting the words, images and experiences that make up our lives. We don't need a science of hermeneutics to be good interpreters any more than we need to know how the digestive system works in order to eat. Nonetheless, just as it's good to have people around (Doctors) who do know how the digestive system works so they can help us when things go wrong so it's sometimes useful to step back from the ongoing business of interpreting to think about interpretation itself and, especially, to think about what makes for a good or an appropriate interpretation.

Although we're increasingly habituated to thinking of language as reducible to bits of information that can be processed by a computer, interpretation remains at the centre of our lives and it is significant that no one has yet managed to reduce interpretation to an exact science. We have already referred to the seminal role of the early nineteenth century theologian Friedrich Schleiermacher with regard to modern theology and here too his contribution was epoch-making. Schleiermacher did more than anyone else to found the modern discipline of hermeneutics, and, interestingly, took pains to define it very deliberately as an *art*. He argued that alongside the very objective discipline of learning the etymology of words and how they relate grammatically there must always be what he called the gift of 'divination'. He described this as the 'feminine' side of interpretation – as opposed to the masculinity of hard, critical analysis and classification – involving the ability to empathise with the very particular nuance of sensibility being expressed. We may not go along with his gender stereotyping – although it certainly wasn't intended to be to the detriment of 'the feminine'.

It should not be difficult to see how hermeneutics has become a vital part of contemporary theology. Perhaps it is worth adding that Schleiermacher, who did so much to create modern hermeneutics, lived in a time when questions about the historical accuracy of the Bible and attempts to reconstruct an historical 'life of Jesus' were first becoming widespread. It is in this context above all that questions of hermeneutics (with or without the word itself) have become so central to theological discussion, because the question 'Is the Bible Still Believable?' cannot be answered without considering the hermeneutical question 'What Does the Bible *Mean*?'. Those who decide that the Bible is not believable because they think if has been proved that at certain key points it is historically inaccurate (or, for that matter, who can only believe it to be true as long as they are able to believe it to be factually correct throughout) have, in fact, already made some very far-reaching hermeneutical assumptions. There are many other ways of reading the Bible as a meaningful document other than those which make meaning dependent on historical accuracy. Indeed, the intensity of the discussion about history and about facts has probably led to a very great impoverishment of our understanding of the Bible, an impoverishment which has made us – fundamentalists and rationalists alive – rather less intelligent interpreters of the scriptures than our ancestors.

Let us look, firstly, at a famous (or, some might say, infamous) modern debate about the interpretation of the Bible, then, bearing in mind the various points of view operative in that debate look at the rather different approach to scripture, widespread in the Middle Ages, known as typology before, finally, looking at the ways in which scripture is 'read' in the context of contemporary liturgy.

The Demythologising Debate

In 1941, with Europe engulfed in war, the Marburg theologian Rudolf Bultmann published an essay entitled 'New Testament and Mythology' in which he argued that it had become necessary to separate the 'kerygma', the 'hard core' of the Christian proclamation, from the first-century mythology in which we find it clothed in the New Testament. In one of the many challenging statements contained in his essay Bultmann declared: 'It is impossible to use electric light and the wireless and to avail ourselves of modern medical and surgical discoveries, and at the same time to believe in the New Testament world of spirits and miracles.'[1]

This was not, of course, the first instance in modern times of the New Testament being described as 'mythological'. In a massive study *The Life of Jesus Critically Examined*, first published in 1835, another German theologian, David Friedrich Strauss (in the view of most of his contemporaries) had appeared to reduce the life of Jesus to an amalgam of first-century Messianic myths. Even before Strauss, there had been a lively debate running through much of the eighteenth century as to how the biblical history could be reconciled with the increasingly stringent demands of historical, philological, geological and physical science. In the seventeenth and early eighteenth centuries Britain had provided some of the most outspoken critics of biblical revelation but by the turn of the nineteenth century it had become relatively conservative. Nevertheless, Strauss's work was soon translated into English (by the novelist, George Eliot) and the issues it raised were contested as hotly here as they were elsewhere in Europe.

One response to historical criticism was to seek to distinguish between the essential core of Christian teaching and the husk of dogma and doctrine that had grown up around it. In a highly influential series of lectures delivered in the Winter Term of 1899–1900 (and published as *What is Christianity?*) another German theologian, Adolf Harnack, had argued that the teaching of Jesus could be summed up in three essential points: (1) the Kingdom of God; (2) the Fatherhood of God and the value of the human soul; (3) the commandment of love.

Harnack stressed the simplicity and accessibility of this message, that it was truly something 'available for all'. But what, many Christians might ask, of the redemptive aspect of the gospel? What about the saving and atoning value of Christ's sacrificial death? What about the resurrection? What about the doctrine of the Son of God 'of the Father's love begotten, ere the world began to be'? Harnack is unambiguous: these things are all part of the 'husk' that grew up to protect or to help pass on the gospel – but in doing so distorted it. In the course of the debate over the person of Christ, Harnack wrote, 'men put an end to brotherly fellowship for the safe of a *nuance*, and thousands were cast out, condemned, loaded with chains and done to death. It is a gruesome story. On the question of "Christology" men beat their religious doctrines into terrible weapons, and spread fear and intimidation everywhere.' Jesus himself, by way of contract, 'desired no other belief in his person and no other attachment to it than is contained in the keeping of his commandments.'[2] What we can say of Jesus is simply this: that he knew God as his Father to a degree unparalleled elsewhere, but,

> How he came to this consciousness of the unique character of his relation to God as a Son ... is his secret, and no psychology will ever fathom it ... We are not even able to say when it was that he first knew himself as the Son, and whether he at once completely

identified himself with this idea and let his individuality be absorbed in it, or whether it formed an inner problem which kept him in constant suspense.[3]

Bultmann, however, went far beyond this. In his view it was not just the time-bound historical 'husk' of the New Testament message that had become strange to us nor was it enough to find new words in which to dress old and familiar thoughts. His aim was, rather, to translate the New Testament *out of* the thought-world of the first century and into the thought-world of modern times. For him, this meant using the language and the concepts of existentialist philosophy. For example, he can say that the meaning of faith is 'to open ourselves freely to the future' or to find 'authentic self commitment'; or that what the New Testament calls living 'according to the flesh' can be seen in terms of 'anxiety' or 'self-assertion'. What this meant to Bultmann's critics was that he was reducing the gospel to the demand for a mere shift in human attitudes and that the aim of Christian proclamation was fulfilled whenever any hearer of the Word made the move from 'self-assertion' to 'self-commitment'. Although Bultmann himself went on insisting that this transformation was only possible on the basis of a prior act of God he seemed to many to dispense with such essential 'facts' as the Virgin Birth, miracles, the Resurrection, etc. There didn't seem to be any scope left for 'acts of God' outside the world of purely human psychological experiences. 'Faith' was simply having a changed attitude to life – rather than a changed attitude to life being merely one result (amongst others) of 'believing in' Jesus as historically and factually Risen Lord and Saviour. Some of Bultmann's more radical followers were, indeed, quite happy to go down this road and to re-cast Christianity as a purely human event (though nonetheless distinctive over against, for example, scientific humanism).

All this may seem to be but a slight variation on Harnack's project of detaching the timeless truth of the gospel from the shell of the particular historical circumstances in which it first saw the light of day. But there are important differences that have to do with Bultmann's very radical view of history. As he sees it, human life is from beginning to end caught up in the never-ending flow of history. This historical character of the human being 'does not consist in the fact that he is an individual who passes through history, who experiences history, who meets with history. No, man is nothing but history ... Man is only a process ...'[4] The consequence, it would seem is that all 'truths' are historically relative and that the historical process is without purpose or goal. Bultmann thus stares into an abyss of relativism and nihilism that Harnack could scarcely have fathomed. Even the 'hard core' of Jesus's teaching as described by Harnack turns out to be inseparable from history – the history of Jesus's own time, on the one hand, and the history of the interpreter (his own background and training), on the other. Even the quest for timeless truths standing aloof from the cut and thrust of historical reality is itself a distinctively modern preoccupation! Bultmann, by way of contrast, looked to a transformation of existential attitudes that is always shaped differently by the different circumstances of those who experience it.

We can follow the difference between Bultmann and his predecessors further by looking at another important essay, 'Is Exegesis without Presuppositions Possible?'[5] In this essay he argued that our reading of the Bible is always conditioned by he questions we bring to it. As a historian himself Bultmann certainly believed that we should approach the Bible (like any document) with as unprejudiced an eye as possible. Even so, we cannot help reading the text in the light of the 'life-relation' and 'pre-understanding' we bring to it. Thus, he claimed, such forms of 'the question concerning God' as 'the question concerning "salvation", or escape from death, or certainty in the face of a constantly shifting destiny, or truth in the midst of a world that is a riddle to him' will inevitably shape the way in which we experience the text as religiously significant. For example, one period (let us say the late Middle Ages, the time of the Black Death) will find that its religious horizons are shaped almost exclusively by the fear and terror of death whilst another period (let us say the immediate post-War period in Europe) will be more preoccupied by the feeling that all the trusted traditions and institutions have lost their meaning and value. Or – and this is simply to extend Bultmann's argument – the gospel will not be received by dispossessed and oppressed peoples in the Third World today unless it is seen to address issues of social justice, whilst Western Europeans are more likely to be in search of personal security and certainty in a world of endless change. Nineteenth century liberals saw Jesus as an enlightened teacher of morals; twentieth century Africans see him as a Black Liberator. In Bultmann's phrase 'The understanding of the text is never a definitive one, but rather remains open because the meaning of the Scriptures discloses itself anew in every future.'

In the same way that we argued in a previous chapter that Christianity is, in a sense, simply what we make it, so we might say here that the Bible 'means' whatever we understand it as 'meaning'. Let us just go back briefly to the conversation-model of interpretation: the way in which the conversation develops decides how we understand one another and what we make of one another. If in talking to my friends I hide certain facts about myself and draw attention to others; if I speak of myself with humour or pride or avoid speaking of myself altogether – in these and innumerable other happenstances of the communication process I reveal (knowingly or, more often, unknowingly) who I am, eliciting favourable or unfavourable responses as the case may be. One could say, even more strongly, that I not only reveal, I actually determine the character, the sort of person I am, by what I say and by how I say it. In the same way, the implication of Bultmann's argument seems to be that the meaning of the Bible emerges out of the process whereby it is read, preached, quoted, translated, used and abused.

Critics were not slow to point out that this has certain consequences for his own proposals: for if we apply this principle to Bultmann's picture of a demythologised Christianity we can, of course, say that this in turn represents only one possible way of appropriating the meaning of the Bible and that the meaning of the Bible can no more be tied to one particular twentieth century philosophy than it can to the cosmology of the first century. The relativizers get relativized!

Paradoxically this negative-seeming conclusion can begin to open up some interesting constructive possibilities. For if

Bultmann himself seems to be trapped in a curiously funda-
mentalistic prejudice (namely, that there is only one 'true'
interpretation of the gospel for our time), we are now
reaching a point from which we can see that there have
been and are many other readings that might be worthy
of our attention. A conversation, after all, is not an argument
in a law court. It does not aim to capture a single and
incontrovertible view of 'truth' but goes rambling around
innumerable highways and byways, looking at things from a
continually changing sequence of angles. Or, to recall our
other model of remembering the world of childhood experiences, the view I have of my childhood at age twenty is
neither more nor less true than the view I am likely to have at
age forty; the one might be more vivid, the other more
generous – neither is 'right' or 'wrong'. On the contrary,
what my childhood 'means' emerges only in the overall
course of my life.

The implications of this for our present discussion can be
put in the form of a question: instead of tying the debate
about the meaning of the Bible to a confrontation between
the first and twentieth centuries, why not look around a bit
and compare and contrast how we read the Bible now with
other readings that have appeared in the course of the
Church's history. In other words, instead of trying to whittle
the message down into the smallest workable format, why
not allow our minds to expand, to wander, to explore? To
illustrate what might happen if we did just that, let's look at
a kind of interpretation that held sway for much of Christian
history, a kind of interpretation that is most readily flagged
by the terms 'allegory' and 'typology'.

A Type of Reading

The so-called 'allegorical' interpretation of Scripture dominated much of Christian history from the time of the Early
Church down to the beginning of the modern period. In the
twentieth century, however, it has all but vanished. In terms
of our model of evolution it might be regarded as an extinct
species, a theological equivalent of the mammoth or the
pterodactyl! We hope to show, however, that within the

ecological whole of the Church such a type of reading can still yield significant insights into the meaning of Scripture.

The enormity of the revolt against allegory and typology is well-illustrated by a near-classic passage from an English contemporary of Bultmann's, C. H. Dodd (one of the guiding lights of the New English Bible). His study of *The Parables of the Kingdom* opens with a historian's devastating critique of Augustine's allegorical reading of the parable of the Good Samaritan. Dodd has to do little more than quote Augustine in order to have him laughed out of court. Thus:

> *A certain man went down from Jerusalem to Jericho*: Adam himself is meant; *Jerusalem* is the heavenly city of peace, from whose blessedness Adam fell; *Jericho* means the moon, and signifies our mortality, because it is born, waxes, wanes, and dies. *Thieves* are the devil and his angels. *Who stripped him*, namely, of his immortality; *and beat him*, by persuading him to sin ...[6]

Dodd comments: 'To the ordinary person of intelligence who approaches the Gospels with some sense for literature this mystification must appear quite perverse.' (p. 13) None of us, of course, would wish to appear unintelligent and most of us believe we have 'some sense for literature', so what can we say! (Bultmann is similarly dismissive, saying of the allegorical approach that 'it only lets [the text] say what [the interpreter] already knows'.) We do not, however, need to defend Augustine at every point in order to feel some hesitation in proceeding to ditch wholesale a method of interpretation that (as Dodd himself acknowledges in connection with Mark 4.11–20) has roots in the Bible itself. Rather than trying to argue out the fundamental principles involved, let us take a couple of examples of typological interpretation, and show how this method can open up important and compelling readings of the scriptures.

These examples come from the so-called *Biblia Pauperum*, an illustrated medieval work which originated in the late thirteenth century and which became popular throughout French- and German-speaking Europe in the course of the Middle Ages.[7] Recent studies show that it influenced much Church art: for instance a misericord in Ripon cathedral and a stained glass window at St Martin's Church, Stamford

(Lincolnshire) which both show Samson carrying off the Gates of Gaza are closely modelled on the same scene as depicted in one particular edition of the *Biblia*. At a deeper level the overall scheme of the *Biblia* can be traced extensively in such varied works of Church art as the Flemish tapestries of Rheims Cathedral, the windows of King's College, Cambridge and even Michaelangelo's Sistine Chapel ceiling. These few examples indicate that what we are dealing with here is an interpretation of the Bible that is fully representative of the medieval vision.

But what exactly is this book? It exists in a number of versions, but typically it has the following structure: There are forty pages, each page showing three main pictures. The central pictures are (usually) taken from the New Testament and tell the story of redemption from the Annunciation through to the Last Judgement. These images are framed by two other scenes, usually from the Old Testament or the Apocrypha, which can be 'read' as prefiguring or foreshadowing the New Testament scheme in question. These Old Testament scenes are understood as 'types' of the New Testament 'antitype', and thus the whole system of interpretation is known as 'typology'. The relationship between 'type' and 'antitype' is not rigid but varies considerably. In some cases it is an essentially contrasting relationship, in others it is more complementary. Thus, Eve being tempted by the Serpent is used as a contrasting type of the Annunciation, whereas the feeding of the Israelites with Manna is used as a complementary type of the Last Supper. Taken as a whole, however, it is clear that the *Biblia* presents us with a coherent reading of the central saving events of the New Testament message: it is not simply an accumulation of ingenious and arbitrarily connected parallels. The coherence of the *Biblia*'s reading of the Bible is underlined by the way in which each page also contains a prose paraphrase of the story in each of the Old Testament scenes, plus a number of scriptural texts and devotional sentences that help the reader understand the connection between the pictures, in other words, that help us to understand the spiritual meaning of the whole group of images. Indeed, its very purpose may have had the unified aim, given the fact that it typically ran to forty pages, of serving as a daily meditation for Lent.

The first group of images we shall look at here are those that show the baptism of Christ. The two Old Testament scenes used to illustrate this are both taken from the Exodus cycle of stories, one showing the Israelites crossing the Red Sea (with Pharaoh and his army being overwhelmed by the incoming waters in the background) and the other showing the spies, Joshua and Caleb, returning from their reconnaissance mission to the promised land with a sample of its produce – a massive bunch of grapes suspended from a pole carried between them. Let us hear how the *Biblia* itself explains the relevance of these two images:

> According to Exodus xiv, when Pharaoh was following the Israelites with chariots and horsemen, he went after the Israelites into the Red Sea, and the Lord brought back the waters of the sea over them. In this way he freed his people from the hand of the pursuing enemy. In the same way he has even now freed the Christian people from the bonds of Original Sin, by the waters of baptism made holy by Christ.
>
> According to Numbers xiii 1–28 (and xiv 6–7), when the scouts sent to spy out the promised land came back, they cut a cluster of grapes, carried it over a pole, and crossing the Jordan, brought the cluster back as evidence of the richness of that land. This signifies that if we wish to enter the kingdom of heaven we must first pass through the waters of baptism.

There is a very obvious difference between these two types in that the Red Sea type is rooted in the New Testament itself (1 Cor. 10. 1–2: 'For I do not want you to be ignorant, my brothers, that our forefathers were all under the cloud and that they all passed through the sea. They were all baptised into Moses in the cloud and in the sea ...') and has remained 'live' in Christian tradition by its use in rites of baptism. Nevertheless, the familiarity of the common motif of 'deliverance through water' should not dull us to the boldness of this particular juxtaposition.

The use of the story of the two spies, however, is both unexpected and startling. The summary of the incident given in the *Biblia* itself invites us to focus on the motif of the river, that is, the fact that the spies journeyed back through the

Jordan, so that their return to the Israelite assembly can be read as a 'coming-up-out-of-the-water' bearing the promise (or even the first-fruits) of the long-awaited fulfilment of the people's journey. Taken together with the deliverance at the Red Sea this suggests that Christ's baptism is not merely a necessary submission to the requirements of righteousness in an external sense (as could, for instance, be suggested by Matt. 3.16) but is itself a saving event, the beginning of the kingdom being opened to all believers as, through baptism, it still is for each individual believer. In the way in which it anticipates Christ's baptism the return of the spies thus also throws light on baptism in the Church – in the words of the devotional gloss given by the *Biblia* 'the river is crossed and the land of honey is approached'.

But this is not the end of the story. For if the story of the spies is not the kind of story we would naturally associate with Christ's baptism it is also true that the Middle Ages themselves were more accustomed to associate it with another moment of Christ's earthly existence: the Passion. In another well-known medieval typological scheme, the altarpiece of the Church of Klosterneuburg in Austria, the story is given, along with the sacrifice of Isaac as a type of the Crucifixion! The symbolism of this particular type plays on a number of allusions and references in the picture. Firstly, of course, is the imagery of the grapes themselves, recalling (for Christian readers) Jesus's own use of vine imagery, 'I am the true Vine' – imagery which is deeply and extensively founded on the prophetic use of vine-culture imagery to speak to Yahweh's relation to his people. (The most extreme application of vine-associated imagery to the interpretation of the New Testament is the once-popular use of the drunkenness of Noah to illustrate the passion.) Then, less obviously, the image of the wooden pole is used to evoke the wood of the cross (the verse inscribed beneath the image on the Klosterneuburg altar itself runs: 'Read in the pole the wood of the cross, In the grape the sign of Christ'). Avril Henry offers a number of other associations known in the Middle Ages:

> ... the leading figure is the spiritually blind who cannot see Christ, turning their back on him, and the second figure is those

with Christ in front of them, as in Matt. xvi. 24: 'If anyone wants to come after me let him take up his cross and follow'. [Elsewhere] ... it echoes the Carrying of the Cross ; [To] Augustine ... the grapes also represent Christ supported by Old and New Testaments.

Some of these detailed allusions may seem to fall all too easily under the strictures of historical interpreters, but the connection of vine-imagery with the passion is profoundly Biblical. Think of the symbolism of the Eucharist itself or of the 'cup' of suffering which Jesus prays his Father to spare him. So too is the extension of such imagery to baptism, as when Jesus asks James and John 'Can you drink the cup that I drink or be baptised with the baptism that I am baptised with?' (Mark 10.38) or when Paul asks his Roman readers, 'Don't you know that all of us who were baptised into Christ Jesus were baptised into his death?' (Romans 6.3) Similarly, the wood of the cross is a recurrent motif in Christian (if not biblical) thought, as in the legend that identifies the wood of the cross with the wood of the Tree of Knowledge (the instrument of the fall).

The image of the spies' return in this way opens up a rich seam of symbolic devotional themes for those using the *Biblia* for their Lenten meditations. It does not merely play around with somewhat abstract speculative identifications but directs the reader to central doctrinal issues – and raises the question as to how we ourselves are to appropriate the meaning of the biblical text in baptism and in suffering discipleship.

The *Biblia*'s treatment of the Risen Christ's encounter with Mary Magdalene similarly exploits two very different types. The first is that of Daniel in the Lion's Den, more specifically the moment when the King comes back in the morning after the prophet's overnight ordeal and finds Daniel still alive (indeed, with three of the lions playing with him according to the *Biblia*'s artist). The concept of a miraculous deliverance from a mortal trial provides a fairly straightforward complement to the resurrection. At one level the second type is also fairly straightforward, if unexpected. Again, the *Biblia*'s own paraphrase may serve to introduce it:

According to the Canticle of Canticles iii, 1–4, when the betrothed woman had found her beloved she said: 'I have found him whom my soul loves' and then: 'I shall hold him again and not let him go'. This betrothed woman signifies Mary Magdalene who, seeing her beloved (that is, Christ) wanted to hold him. He answered her in this way: 'Do not touch me, for I have not yet ascended to my father'.

The message is further hammered home by another devotional gloss: 'Now the betrothed enjoys the beloved whom she had desired and sought.' By seeing the encounter between Jesus and Mary through the lens of the Song of Songs, in itself a beautiful celebration of the erotic love uniting bride and groom, we are being invited to become aware of the erotic dimension of that relationship, of the quality of passion, of longing desire, which binds this woman disciple (called 'loyal Mary' in the *Biblia*) to Jesus. The previous page of the *Biblia* had used the same Old Testament source in exploring the meaning of Mary's disconsolate search for the body of Christ, glossed as 'This holy woman prays while she diligently looks for her lover [or spouse/groom]'. This is a dimension to which popular contemporary interpretations of the gospels (such as *Godspell* or *Jesus Christ, Superstar*) have not hesitated to draw attention and there need be no implication of cheapness or smut in recognising it. It would be entirely in accordance with his prophetic persona if Jesus was, in an extended sense of the word, 'sexy', that is, having qualities of affective charisma which heightened the all-round emotional charge of situations in which he became involved, inspiring love and hate, discipleship and scandal.

In remarking all this there is no question of forgetting that, for the Middle Ages, the Song of Songs was not read in a straightforward way, but as an allegory of spiritual eros, of the soul's quest for mystical union with Christ. This interpretation is alluded to in the *Biblia*'s pictorial representation of the scene, for the groom is shown not as Solomon but as Jesus himself. It is not an 'earthly' but a 'heavenly' marriage that is afoot here. Nonetheless, there is also a sense in which, given this allegorization, the way in which the *Biblia* uses both word and image to some extent re-eroticizes the scene, re-awakens us to the fact that even the desire for 'spiritual marriage' with Christ (a desire that men as well as women can experience) must involve a full engagement of all our emotional powers. It must be fully human *at least* if it is going to be able to claim to be 'heavenly' as well. The subtle interplay between eros and sublimation in both the scene itself and its interpretation via the Song of Songs can be sensed in the citation of the bride's words from the Song, 'I held him, I shall not let him go' alongside Jesus's words to Mary, 'Do not hold on to me, for I have not yet returned to the father'. The desire which Mary must surrender in ceasing to cling to the Risen Lord must be *at least* as forceful as the desire which makes the human lover refuse to let go of the beloved.

Instead of typology merely offering the reader pre-packaged 'answers' or 'explanations' it can, in these and in innumerable other instances, be shown to open up rich seams of meaning and association, of enquiry and reflection, that readers are then left to meditate on and to appropriate spiritually according to the depth and clarity of their spiritual insight and vigour. With these comments in mind we might go back and re-read Augustine's commentary on the Good Samaritan in a more generous light. Of course, Jesus did not intend each of the specific identifications Augustine makes ('A certain man' = Adam, Jerusalem = the Heavenly City, Jericho = our mortality, etc.). Still, if we recapture the spirit of medieval *meditatio* we might come to see Augustine's re-telling of the story as highlighting the way in which even a simple tale such as this (all-too-familiar in the twentieth century as in the first) can also be the existential story of 'Everyman' – as, perhaps, every good story is – and, as such, it both belongs to and reveals the hidden theological depth-structure of the much larger story of redemption in which it is set.

We may seem to have moved far from the polemics of the demythologising debate, but in one sense the questions that guide us remain remarkably similar. The literary critic Northrop Frye wrote of typology that:

> ... it is a figure of speech that moves in time: the type exists in the past and the antitype in the present, or the type exists in the present and the antitype in the future. What typology really is as

a mode of thought, what it both assumes and leads to, is a theory of history, or more accurately of historical process: an assumption that there is some meaning and point to history ... that despite apparent confusion, even chaos, in human events, nevertheless those events are going somewhere and indicating something ...[8]

He also called it 'existential' in 'the sense of anchoring an interest in the transcendental in the seabed of human concern.'[9] In this way it may very well serve as a creative response to the kind of anxiety about the complete relativity of historical existence that Bultmann articulated. But rather than trying to pin history down to some timeless, a-historical truth, typology works towards meaning in history by stitching together events and moments in time, working out patterns, tendencies and connections, spinning a story that we ourselves are part of and, indeed, that we are responsible for taking further.

It would be interesting to take this discussion further and to see to what extent the typological pattern of thought is, historically, rooted in the Bible itself; in other words, not merely to ask whether typology can help us find unexpected treasures in the Bible but whether the Bible itself, in whole or in part, uses typology. Examples suggesting a positive answer might include: Stephen's speech in Acts 7, the contrast between Adam and Christ in Romans 5.14, Paul's use of Red Sea imagery in relation to baptism in 1 Corinthians 10.1–4 and The Letter to the Hebrews with its lengthy discussion of Christ's sacrifice and priesthood in relation to the Temple ritual of Old Testament religion – but these are only a beginning.

Let us return momentarily to the image of conversation. What makes for a good conversation? Certainly not a situation in which only one speakers holds the stage, reducing everyone else to silence! Yet it has been the tendency of both fundamentalist and revisionist interpreters to try to do just that in the case of biblical interpretation. The point of focusing on medieval typology is not to say that this is what we must all go back to but is, firstly, to allow other voices to be heard in the debate about interpretation; and, secondly it is to encourage us to move beyond the strict letter of the text, to rediscover the freedom to explore novel and even (at first glance) somewhat odd associations and allusions, to re-tell the familiar stories in unfamiliar ways, so as to allow the conversation to move us on from where we were yesterday to where we might be tomorrow. It helps us to see how the Bible itself is involved in the process of tradition and in the Church's self-transforming life. In other words, the return of typology itself can be a creative and not merely nostalgic return to the past. It can indeed be a return that, paradoxically, opens a path into the future.

The Bible in the Liturgy

We should not need to argue for the importance of biblical interpretation for liturgy. The differing readings of the Bible that different generations of Christians have given have shaped and re-shaped what happens in worship in innumerable ways. We have only to think how the Protestant principle of *sola scriptura* transformed not only what happens during worship but the very internal fabric of the Church building – look at the difference between a Methodist Chapel and an Anglican Church. Nor is it coincidental that the abandonment of typological interpretation – a system (or group of systems) of interpretation that has been an almost infinitely fecund source of Christian art should coincide with a move (even in Catholic circles) to a more restrained approach to Church decoration. At a somewhat different level every reformation in the Church is accompanied by a reappraisal of such basic liturgical requisites as lectionaries and the use of texts in liturgies. Thus, the Prayer Book of Edward VI, in its commitment to unmediated biblicism, simply divided its lections up by chapters, so that each day each lesson was simply a whole chapter of scripture, no matter how short or how long. Such an arrangement, of course, ignores the fact that the 'chapters' are not, so to speak, native to the text and do not always coincide with the more significant shifts in subject matter. So, even such a 'raw' presentation of scripture in liturgy is already loaded with implications for how we read the text.

At the other extreme, the one hundred and ten pages of lections in *The Alternative Service Book 1980*, provide a highly sophisticated pre-packaging of scripture, in which thematic groupings predominate over the Reformation attempt simply to give the whole Bible to congregations (or at least to clergy) every year. (It is interesting that by introducing regular Old Testament readings at the Eucharist the revisers have, however minimally, re-opened the door to typological interpretation in the liturgical use of scripture: see, for example, the readings for Easter 1.) There is no doubt that this extensive prior arrangement of scripture will determine to a very considerable degree the experience and understanding of scripture that congregations using it will have, even if it is supplemented by private devotional reading of the Bible, a point on which Free Church members are always ready to prod the consciences of their Anglican brothers and sisters. Yet it would seem that the promotion of a very 'open' approach to interpretation, as outlined in this chapter, would encourage us to regard such a foreclosing of options with some hesitation, to say the least! For it would seem to stop the conversation that is the history of interpretation at a particular and somewhat arbitrary moment in time. This is not to deny the value of such a systematic approach to the reading of scripture in Church. As in so many other areas of liturgy, however, what is valuable as a tool should not be allowed to become a straitjacket. Of course, if there is going to be any kind of 'Church year' some regular ordering of lections is almost inevitable. The question is, simply, how far to go.

A remarkable contemporary approach to reading the Bible in the context of liturgy – and one that seems equally remote from the worlds of demythologising, typology and the ASB – is the kind of participatory experiment initiated by Ernesto Cardenal (later to be minister of culture in Nicaragua's Sandinista government) when he was parish priest to the island community of Solentiname, a community made up of poorly educated peasants and fisherfolk. Sometimes in and sometimes out of Church, sometimes even in the context of the mass, Cardenal opened up the interpretation of scripture to his congregation. Instead of a sermon, the Bible reading would be followed by a discussion. As Cardenal himself notes:

> Not all of those who attended mass shared in the discussion to the same degree. Others nearly always had something to say. Marcelino is a mystic. Olivia a theologian. Rebeca, Marcelino's wife, always speaks about love. Laureano relates everything to the revolution. Eblis thinks only of the perfect society of the future. Felipe, another of the young men, thinks above all of the struggle of the oppressed classes. Old Tomás, his father, cannot read, yet speaks with great wisdom.[10]

Certainly, as we read through these discussions we soon learn to anticipate the kind of approach that any particular speaker is going to take! It is astonishing (or perhaps not) that within this narrow, isolated rural community such a range of nuanced readings of the Bible emerge so quickly and so naturally – albeit all (or nearly all) of them fall within the parameters of liberation theology (that is, theology committed to the struggle for social justice).

Yet, if this example seems too exotic, there are perhaps many Church communities in Britain today (and not only among house Churches or in newly planted Churches) where, especially in the increasing number of informal family services, a similar freedom is being exercised with regard to the Bible in worship. So, perhaps, a dramatic presentation might replace an actual reading, or a single reading be made the focus of the service rather than a carefully construed layering of readings (with the inevitable pre-determination of meaning that must go along with that). This is not to say that all such experiments work, nor even that they are desirable *every* week: it is simply to note that they are happening and to suggest that there are ways in which that kind of freedom can, from time to time, inform our more formal worship as well. Everything must depend on what is appropriate in the particular circumstances of particular Churches, bearing in mind local traditions, the level of consensus and not losing sight of the wider body of which the local Church is a part.

Such freedom can help us to discover what the message of the Bible means for us, as communities as well as individuals. It can help us to break away from those models which see the 'truth' of the bible as being fixed once-for-all 'behind' the

text and consequently to get the debate about the meaning of
the Bible out into the actual life of the Church. It can also
help us to put to good use the model of conversation developed at the start of this chapter as we share with the Church
of the past in the continual labour and play of interpreting.
For it is in this labour and in this play alone that 'the
meaning' of the Bible comes to light, bringing inspiration,
challenge and judgement. In Nicaragua and in rural England
alike the human imagination proves itself to be as creative
and as fertile in producing striking and illuminating interpretations of Scripture as it was in the ages that saw the
flowering of typological schemes. Through interpretation,
then, the Bible itself participates in the process of Spirit-and-
tradition that is the life of the Church.

Yet there will be those (though many of them may have
already thrown their hands up in despair!) who will argue
that such a model is not adequate to the claims of 'truth' that
Christians make for and on behalf of the biblical message.
They will object that in a conversation 'anything goes', and
everyone's word is as good as anyone else's. On such a model
all authority, all consensus in the Church would be destroyed
in a flash. But we do not need to accept the severity of this
view of 'conversation'. Of course, it is true that bad conver-
sations happen in which, for instance, the different voices
just talk past each other and fail to connect. But it is just as
bad if there is really only one voice speaking. Genuine
conversation involves a willingness to listen and a lively
interest in the views of the other speakers – as well as a readi-
ness to express one's own position in as interesting and as
appropriate a form as one can. Neither arrogance nor false
modesty will do. We might add that the style of Jesus's own
ministry was, in certain key respects, 'conversational'.
Although there were clearly occasions when he simply delivered a teaching there are other occasions when the teaching
emerges out of the conversation he has with others, as, for
example, in the case of the Syro-phoenician woman, whose
words (rather than the words of Jesus) deliver the story's
punch-line. It is the argument of this chapter that when the
Bible is interpreted by the Church in this 'conversational'
mode – a mode which will encourage us to listen again to

other interpretations and other voices than those which have dominated the theological debates of recent times – then that is when it will best help us to discover what our faith means to us. For the Bible as we know it is essentially the written record of the Church's conversation with itself in the times of its greatest creative activity and life, the times of revelation. In our reading and re-reading of the Bible our time can also become such a time of revelation.

Chapter 5

Ecumenism and the Meeting of Traditions

Sicilian Vespers

Sicilian and English culture have surprisingly more in common than expectations might allow. The influence of the Normans is the most significant piece of shared tradition, and even the untrained eye can identify the unmistakably Romanesque arcading in the Palatine Chapel in Palermo, reflecting patterns often identified in the churches of Norman England. The vibrancy of contemporary Sicilian culture is in profound contrast, however, to the cooler and more detached atmosphere of Britain and the rest of Northern Europe. Mad dogs and Englishmen may well venture out in the Sicilian midday sun, but they will almost certainly not venture to express their emotions with the immediacy characteristic of the local inhabitants of Palermo, Messina or elsewhere in this volcanic Mediterranean island.

Understandably such cultural patterns surface too in the local religion. A brief story sets the scene. The archiepiscopal party had robed in the Cardinal's residence and we were then bidden to cross the road to the Cathedral where we would worship. As we left the cloistered courtyard of the residence and turned left into the narrow street, we found ourselves facing upwards of two hundred Roman Catholic priests, flanking us on the right and on the left. This ecclesiastical guard of honour presaged greater things to come. The expansive Cathedral opened up before us and it was packed with people throughout. The faithful sang hymns and chants, as the Archbishop and Cardinal and their parties made their way to the sanctuary. There were, we gathered later, more than four thousand people there – rather more than the average for an English ecumenical service during the Week of Prayer for Christian Unity. We were treated to Solemn Vespers. The pattern of the Office was there for all to see. Psalms, scripture and antiphons offered us the integrity of evening prayer. But it was unmistakably not Anglican Evensong. Near the climax of the service was the imposition of incense. A censer was set before the Archbishop of Canterbury, the lid of which had the proportion of a sizeable medieval gothic font cover; the Archbishop was obscured from the congregation's view by this remarkable thurible, as he put on incense and blessed it. This great instrument was then placed in the hands of the Cardinal, who censed the altar, the Archbishop, and the people and the service then continued following a similar pattern with which it had begun.

None of the English people amongst us present had ever experienced ecumenical worship quite like this before. Something of the conventional mixture was admittedly there. An Adventist, a Methodist and an Anglican lay woman read lessons; representationalism has infected even the heart of the Latin ecclesiastical world. But this was about all that was familiar to us. The emotion – we were almost mobbed on our exit from the Cathedral as the Archbishop and the Cardinal blessed the people during the recessional – was powerful and electrifying in its effect. The liturgy was beautiful, moving and well performed – even the most exotic Anglo-Catholicism could not have produced the atmosphere or indeed quite the Latin sense of theatre. Finally the popular piety was a world apart from the more cerebral word-based religion that we know even in the more catholic corners of northern Europe save perhaps the Republic of Ireland. The tradition had taken root in people's hearts.

Diversity in Unity

The lesson that we learnt is not to be forgotten, for it reaches to the heart of ecumenical endeavour. There was the pattern of the office, there were prayers which we share and a indeed a common scripture. That gave us the confidence to worship with all our hearts. But that which excited us and which took us a further step along the road in understanding our own tradition and in feeling a sense of the wider river of which we are but one current, was that in which we differed. It was the diversity, the remarkable, and the unusual in the worship which both touched our hearts and our understanding. The tradition of which we know we are a part is not static nor undifferentiated. Indeed rather like the insights which science has gained from the laws of entropy, that is of increasing disorder, so we discovered something similar here. The tradition is a living expression of our faith. As such it will ever be broadening and finding new modes of expression. We should not be surprised to find that this has been the case down the centuries and indeed as we encounter different cultures.

It is not clear that ecumenical enthusiasts or the churches themselves have yet fully discovered this or at least they certainly do not seem to have taken it to heart. Often the experience of ecumenical worship is dire, and most particularly so when we try too hard. The exotic and the distinctive are banned. Living traditions are abandoned and instead an *ersatz* tradition is sought. It will be inoffensive, unattractive, and inauthentic because it does not exist outside that one passing moment. The same truth could so easily spill over into our theological dialogue and our co-operative mission if we are not more aware of these dangers. Only living tradition will support further life.

It is common knowledge that the mention of ecumenical relationships between churches is capable either of stimulating remarkable excitement upon the face of others or indeed of provoking a sustained and heartfelt yawn. Since the Edinburgh Conference of 1910, remarkable changes have taken place in the relationships between the Christian Churches. The ecumenical movement, standing alongside the allied liturgical movement has contributed remarkable energy to the Church and it has also lead to a radical re-appraisal of tradition. Dialogue between the different Christian Churches has begun from a number of different starting points. For some it was the pressing need for the churches to contribute more effectively and powerfully towards the moral formation of the contemporary world. So was born the Life and Work Movement and so was born too the strong commitment of many ecumenists to social change. For others the stimulus to work for unity came from the need to proclaim a common gospel rooted in an agreed faith and delivered to the world by ministers from different churches who could recognise the validity of each other's orders. Herein lie the roots of the Faith and Order Movement. The Liturgical Movement has itself been a further stimulus towards unity. Liturgical scholarship has led people back to appreciate the common patterns of liturgy before the church fragmented at various times in its history.

The other most powerful stimulus towards unity in our day has been the Second Vatican Council. We have already recognised the remarkable changes which it inaugurated in the Roman Catholic Church. No less important are the effects of that Council more widely amongst the Churches. When people now speak of 'a pre-Vatican II' outlook they often refer not simply to Roman Catholics but to what they would see as a more general reactionary or obscurantist point of view. Part of the stimulus for unity which issues from Vatican II arises from the Degree on Ecumenism itself. No longer was the Catholic Church the only true Church. Now the Church subsisted in the Catholic Church but truth was also lived out in different separated Communions. In more recent years much progress has been made in recognising this in regard to the ancient Churches of the East. Considerable progress has also been made in recognising common ground with other Churches, of the Reformation period, which have retained episcopal order and which adhere to a common catholic sacramentality. Much of this progress has been made possible through what has become known almost technically as 'Theological Dialogue'. The dialogue between Anglicans and Roman Catholics[1] is perhaps a classical example. Set up by Archbishop Michael Ramsey and Pope Paul VI in 1966, the dialogue aimed to go behind the polemical controversies of the sixteenth century to seek for a common faith. The results of this search have been remarkable, even if there remain stumbling blocks along the way.[2] By standing back from the earlier controversies and debates it has been possible to discover a common understanding of faith in the areas of ministry and sacraments, the Eucharist and even to some extent authority. One of the keys to these developments was the use of the word *koinonia* or *communion* as a seed around which a new theological understanding could grow. Ecumenical commentators would argue that such communion-based theologies take us back to the heart of the gospel, indeed listening to some of these reflections one very much has in mind the language used by John Henry Newman. The image might again be of a flower unfolding. One could equally argue, however, that the fertile ground discovered by ecumenical theologians has led to a new and dynamic understanding of tradition. Almost imperceptibly a movement has occurred.

The effects of Vatican II have not, of course, been restricted simply to the Decree on Ecumenism. The effect of this instant reformation within Roman Catholicism has been almost like that of an earthquake. For the largest church in Christendom to make such radical changes so swiftly was bound to cause tremors elsewhere. We hinted at that when we discussed Vatican II earlier. One of the other realms in which the effects of the Council have been particularly encouraging has been in the development of liturgy. Catholic theologians have been galvanised to see the implications of change and their own liturgical scholarship has been picked up and indeed added to by scholars of so many different traditions. The world of liturgy and worship is now a quite different place. Furthermore, because of the new understanding of the Church, there has been an intercourse between the traditions undreamed of in an earlier age. As a child I can remember going to a wedding and asking whether a particular aunt would be there. Of course not I was told, Auntie Winnie is a Roman Catholic; she isn't allowed to come to our weddings. The effect of these changes has been felt so much more widely in our understanding and our appreciation of liturgy.

Christian Identity

Reflection upon our experience of different liturgical traditions is perhaps one of the sharpest means of understanding a living and constantly evolving tradition. To take part, for example, in the *Timqat* Rite of the Ethiopian Orthodox Church at the Feast of the Epiphany is to engage with a venerable tradition celebrated for centuries by a church which claims, amongst others, to be the most ancient of the Christian churches. At Timqat, the tabats, or 'arks of the covenant' are carried from their churches to a place where there is water; the next morning the waters are blessed and the tabats return to their churches. It is a great feast and public holiday and to some it will appear more Jewish than Christian. Or again, the fairly frequent use in Ethiopian liturgies of the rhythmic dance-like movements of the numerous deacons as they simultaneously hit the ground with their prayer sticks might appear to have stronger links with the local history and culture of that ancient African country than with what we in the West understand by and have experienced as Christianity. This, combined with a knowledge of the unusual circular ground plan which is essential to Ethiopian churches, including a central section of 'Holy of Holies' which contains the 'ark' and into which the priest only may enter would further fuel the suspicions of the western observer of an eclectic origin to the Ethiopian Christian tradition. The entire polity, liturgy and spirituality of the church is different from anything that European civilisation knows, even taking into account the different traditions of Chalcedonian Orthodoxy and of the other ancient Oriental Orthodox Churches. But the contrast between traditions stretches to further horizons still. Figures estimated recently suggest that there are more priests in the Ethiopian church than there are soldiers in the country's armed forces. For a nation which was engaged in a bloody battle when these figures were calculated, this suggests a different attitude to both deployment and the cult from anything known in mainstream European Christian ecclesiastical culture.

An immediate response from a European observer to these factors would be to criticise Ethiopian Christianity for allowing itself to be formed more by its ambient culture than by the essence of Christianity. Hints at an unreformed, or better perhaps untransformed Judaism, issue from talk of the ark, of the continued practice of circumcision and of the distinction still made between clean and unclean meats. Some of the ritual dance rhythms and other elements of the music in their worship direct one more obviously to the surrounding culture in which the church has been nurtured than to Christianity as western people have experienced it. Talk, however, of the 'essence' of Christianity is in itself not uncontentious. It returns us to Harnack and others in the Liberal Protestant school of the nineteenth century. They believed that the work of the historical theologian was analogous to the work of the art restorer. Layer upon layer of grime, varnish and overpainting could be removed until the 'original' painting was restored to its pristine condition. Having arrived at such a state, then and only then could the painting's original meaning be discerned. This, however, assumes that we have retained the same cultural equipment and understanding through which the painting was origi-nally conceived and later interpreted.

It is far from clear that such cultural equipment is passed on from generation to generation unchanged. A similar fallacy may exist in regard to playing classical music according to its original scoring and on original instruments. The results may well be purifying, cleansing and pleasing to the ear, but we cannot be certain that our experiencing of these sounds, and their aesthetic impact upon us is the same as it would have been for the composer and his or her original hearers. It assumes, as we have argued before, that Christianity can somehow be refined so that at least two and possibly more constitutive elements can be distinguished from each other. First of all there is the original kernel of the gospel and its source in Jesus and his teachings. Then there is the varnish and even the grime which have been added or deposited by the culturally defined developing tradition. It is hazardous to attempt to argue for building such a Christian doctrinal refinery. It is difficult to see, for example, what such an original kernel would have looked like; each indi-vidual hearer of Jesus was bound to have subjected what she or he heard to an interpretation.[3] We cannot ignore the hermeneutical considerations which determine our receiving of the tradition. All this we have discovered already in our earlier reflections upon the Bible and its interpretation, and indeed in our study of Christian doctrinal development or evolution.

Identifying such difficulties in refining the tradition is not, however, to enter upon a road of uncritical relativism. Our reflections upon evolution in doctrine asserted the essential part which is played by continuity in the tradition. Even a mutation must owe its characteristic form and behaviour to its genetic parents. Rather we are arguing, and this is made clear in our understanding of different contemporary traditions within the Christian churches, that the tradition of living and thus healthy faith will change. This change will be encouraged by the energy derived from the Spirit of God. We can even discern the beginnings of such transformations within the different liturgical practices of the present day.

When, in 1990, the then Archbishop of Canterbury visited Bangladesh, the first great gathering for worship with the Church of Bangladesh was a Eucharist. The Church of Bangladesh, like some of the other non-Roman Catholic, non-Orthodox Churches of the Indian sub-continent is of a mixed tradition. It is a 'United Church'. In this case it represents the fairly recent confluence of Anglican, Methodist and Presbyterian traditions. The predominant influence has been one of Anglo-Catholic spirituality, and so the liturgical tradition of the Church of Bangladesh is not only eucharistic, but also fairly ritualistic. This first Eucharist of the Archbishop's visit took place in the Roman Catholic Cathedral in Dhaka. This was the only church of sufficient size to accommodate the congregation. The local Catholic hierarchy were happy for it to be so used, and indeed remarked afterwards on the similarity of the rite to their own liturgy. The liturgy, however, promised some mild surprises for the western European participants. Included within the worship was a Sankey and Moody revivalist hymn translated into Bengali. The language and the rhythm transformed the melody into something recognisable but still quite different from the hymn as sung within western evangelical Christian circles. From a rather different source in the Christian tradition, incense was used at a number of different points during the worship, although at no stage was it placed in a western or indeed in an Orthodox-style censer. Instead, at the beginning and end of the Eucharist, at the gospel and at the offertory, young women, clothed in traditional Bengali dress, swayed their way down the main aisle and into the liturgical space before the altar, moving rhythmically and cradling pottery bowls with burning incense, in their hands.

Once again the rite was recognisably and indeed undeniably Christian, but the seeds of a new and developing tradition were there. In this case style may well, in years to come, influence the precise shape and content of the liturgy. The contrasts with the West are relatively insignificant in comparison with experience of the Ethiopian liturgical tradition. The likelihood of rapid and dramatic change is small, since the Church of Bangladesh in its government, in its antecedents, and in its place within more than one world communion is constrained it to some considerable degree. Where mainstream churches, however, are taking greater risks in the way in which they sew the seeds of the gospel – as for example in some of the new religious communities in parts of Africa – so the scope for the living tradition to develop in quite radically transformed ways increases. This is the force of Vincent Donovan's argument which we quoted earlier.[4]

Cultural Influences

This then identifies yet another aspect of our understanding of a living tradition that repays some further reflection in relation to the different churches and their mutual self understanding. It is commonplace that when Protestants (and to some degree western Roman Catholics) visit an Orthodox country and attend the liturgy there is a profound sense of cultural shock. Services are long – perhaps four hours or more for a celebration of the liturgy – there are numerous and often repeated litanies; few receive communion, and there is almost continuous 'coming and going' within what is experienced by westerners as a liturgical mêlée. Often the music, and even the liturgical drama, are appreciated for their aesthetic content, but the rite seems alien and even irrelevant to many a western eye. How can such a liturgical tradition challenge a people to receive the gospel or proclaim the simple truths of a saving faith?

Alongside this perception, however, runs another and arguably deeper strand. Attending Orthodox worship is often as moving for the western participant, through the opportunity it offers to appreciate the response of the faithful, as it is through the opportunity to experience the music and liturgical drama. There appears to be an almost instinctual response from the hearts of the worshipppers, which is rarely perceived in the mainstream western European traditions. Even those countries which until recently suffered under a repressive totalitarian and avowedly atheistic communist regime have not lost their instinct for Christian worship. To attend the celebration of the liturgy for the Feast of St George, in the Georgian Orthodox Church of St George in the heart of Tbilisi is a profoundly moving experience. The church is in perpetual hubbub and there is a remarkable mixture of the formal and the informal. Even the vesting of the Patriarch, as he begins the rite, within the body of the congregation, retains an air of informal formality. Elderly worshippers appear to cross themselves continuously and automatically at the divine name, the gloria and elsewhere within the liturgy. Icons are kissed by the faithful throughout the rite. Toddlers gaze upwards with trusting eyes, full of faith, appearing as they sing to imbibe a religion which is, from earliest childhood, seen to be both a regular food and nourishment, and which is also part of the 'human dance' which Georgians step out to almost from the moment of their birth.

This tradition, and examples could be multipled from throughout Eastern Europe and the former Soviet Union, stands in contradistinction to the more cerebral and word-centred religion of the Protestant and even Roman Catholic west. There are admittedly parallels in the folk Catholicism of Poland and perhaps even of Ireland. There are also, of course, immediate resonances with the Uniate style, Eastern Rite Catholic Churches. Western Europe has, however, been shaped by a far less experiential and more propositional form of the Christian faith. This has been further strengthened by the experience of the Reformation and the Enlightenment. Undeniably, certain residual elements of an implicit or folk-religion do live on in the rites of passage which are still used by an otherwise largely unchurched majority, but in large tracts of western European civilisation this instinctual religion has been consciously discouraged on intellectual grounds.

So, even to attend an evangelical preaching service in a western European country is to experience an intellectualised form of Christianity, whatever may be the content of the actual message. The Anglican eucharistic rites deriving from the Henrician Reformation are beautiful and pleasing in their lapidary verbosity, but the reasoning behind their shape and composition was unquestionably intellectual in its aims; the express intention of these rites was that they should be participated in and understood fully by the faithful. Similar comments can be even more obviously made in relation to certain of the Lutheran traditions within Europe and Elsewhere. Worshipping, for example on *Himmelfahrt*, that is Ascension Day – even the German name (which means 'Heaven journey') emphasises the centrality of words and their meaning – was to experience profound seriousness in religion. The eucharist was celebrated in the parish church of a medium-sized town in the eastern part of Germany. Until very recently religion had been drastically controlled and discriminated against by the state. The night before we attended this service, we had experienced one parishioner after another telling us of the privations which they had suffered during the rule of the previous regime. Many had lost their jobs, their children had been given poorer schooling, and opportunities for advancement in society were deliberately withheld. At the Eucharist, the pastor, attired in black gown and plain green stole, adverted to some of these facts and pointed to the hope offered through the ascended and glorified Christ. The sermon was well constructed, didactic and hortatory in tone and some thirty minutes in length. The liturgy itself was read with little drama, but in solemn tones, and everyone of us in the church communicated. The contrasted with the scene in Tbilisi is striking although for different reasons the liturgy was equally moving.

This, then, is not to imply that such Protestant worship is devoid of beauty. There is a genuine beauty in simplicity, in the cleanliness and good order of a Lutheran Church interior, not to mention the aesthetic potency of organ preludes and hymn-singing. We might also reflect on the high esteem collectors place on American Shaker furniture – furniture that is simple, functional yet wonderfully graceful. There are, moreover, Lutheran traditions which permit a certain amount of ceremonial such as the use of the chasuble or sacred heart symbolism in Danish Lutheran Churches. Not everything can be fitted into the typically Anglican categories of 'high' and 'low'.

Nonetheless, with these qualifications we may speak of two perceptions of the tradition. If left unrecognised and unresolved these two perceptions of the tradition present difficulties both in appreciating new paths toward ecumenical understanding and in comprehending the nature of the tradition and its appropriation of the Spirit of God. Of course, it would be a gross caricature to see the eastern Christian tradition as rooted purely in the Spirit and in the emotions, through the apparently innate instinct to worship. The Eastern theological and spiritual tradition will not support such a view, which caricatures it as unrelated to the intellectual grounding of Christianity. There is an equal danger in implying that in the West the instinct to worship is absent. Some of the most obviously revivalist traditions in the West, including the Charismatic Renewal Movement, to which we have alluded earlier, are keen to emphasise the significance of religion beginning with the heart and not in the dry canal of a lifeless cerebral formalism. Nevertheless there is the continuing danger of these two elements effectively becoming isolated from each other. For these reasons alone, one can argue for the significance of worship and liturgy as being the point of intersection. Tradition is not simply a body of words, nor is it an unidentifiable series of signals or dramas which have no particular coincidence with the stream of theological reflection which has shaped Christianity in a variety of ways down the centuries.

Liturgy and Tradition

Liturgy and worship then lie central to any understanding of the tradition. The oft-repeated phrase *lex orandi, lex credendi* is essential in this understanding, but it is not as simple as arguing that the law of prayer leads to the law of faith. Instead there is a dialectical relationship which requires each to engage with the other within the life of the Christian community. Worship offers a context for the work of theologians. Worship cannot be used as a means of guarding doctrine from criticism and change. Some indeed have written of the 'hateful change of novelty' and used it as a reason for protecting an unchanging and unchangeable truth.[5] Liturgy has often been the first fortress from which to conduct this battle. For understandable reasons, the Christian community has often been slow to champion liturgical change. The instinct to worship and to respond to particular cultic forms and landmarks in prayer is part of the reason for this. Christian worship is also in one sense inherently conservative, for it is dependent within the Christian tradition on anamnesis; in worship the community remembers the story which is at the heart of its faith. By performing certain sacred dramas, the saving work enshrined in this story is made available to the living community. Through liturgy too the wider tradition of the Church is made present through preaching, prayer, hymnody and the ordering of the Church's year to incorporate the remembrance of significant moments in the continuing history of revelation. Worship is ineluctably a corporate activity and our understanding of a living tradition is thereby protected from a relativising individualism. It is *our* story we repeat, and *my* story and *yours* find themselves resonating with that which we have received.

Nevertheless it is at this very point of common faith and common worship where we most sharply encounter the dilemmas and paradoxes that lie about the path of those who would work for closer relationships between Christian churches. Stephen Sykes has written: 'What is required for the unity of the Church is a coherent family of liturgies with a common character.'[6] Enormous steps have been made in discovering such a 'coherent family of liturgies with a common character'. The fourfold action of the eucharist and the rediscovery of early Christian forms for eucharistic worship, both deriving from the enthusiasm of the liturgical movement, have helped identify patterns which Christian churches have all used in recent revisions of that rite which lies central to the continuing life the community. But as our reflections have indicated it is through that in which we differ most that we see often most encouragingly the living tradition. Do not the common character and the distinctive elements work against each other as we seek to understand the relationship between Spirit and tradition?

The ancient cathedral of Etchmiadzin in Armenia is founded at the place where St Gregory the Illuminator is reputed to have received a vision of the Incarnation. Interestingly, it is built directly above a still more ancient temple to Mithras. The siting of this ancient place of worship identifies the heart of this paradox of the tradition. It is most likely that this site was chosen as much because a Christian church could then replace a pagan temple, as it was because of the vision of St Gregory. In other words, it was a means of establishing the new faith so that it could effectively supplant the old. Yet paradoxically in so doing, the new faith was at least in one sense building upon the foundations of the old. The new tradition of liturgical worship was utterly discontinuous with the old; the Mithraic myth would, as a living religion, fade and die. But still the new faith built its shrine on the foundations of a place where religious traditions had been nourished and had thrived and had fed an earlier community. The tradition that took over from Mithras remains lively and supports a diaspora now spread widely throughout the world. Its liturgical foundations in the eucharist are clearly recognisable but have their own distinctive identity and variations, both in content and performance, which differ widely from any of the traditions rooted in Western Christian culture. This distinctiveness is an integral part of what makes the Armenian tradition attractive.

At this point in history it is difficult to see how this very distinctive tradition could easily find itself united with other Christian communions. As a Christian tradition, it is part of 'a coherent family of liturgies' and to a degree it shares with other traditions a common character, to use the criteria established by Stephen Sykes. For the Armenian liturgy is still undoubtedly and recognisably built upon the same foundations as the eucharist which we know in the west.

Nevertheless the very distinctive ethnic and cultural foundations which mark off the identity of the Armenian Apostolic Orthodox Church, both in its country of origin and within its diaspora, mean that its living tradition will almost by definition continue to exhibit a distinctive, even if eventually developing, character.

The meeting of traditions, then, within Christianity indicates once again the presence of the same themes which we have identified elsewhere in these chapters. Over the centuries, the Spirit within the different traditions has led the varied parts of the Christian Church to express both doctrine and liturgical practice in a great variety of ways. Perhaps one of the key lessons offered by the ecumenical movement relates to how we can learn to accept that all of these variations are somehow part of the Christian tradition, and that that tradition in itself cannot easily be refined to identify that which was the kernel from which all began. Seeking that kernel in the past has always developed into a search for the elusive, seeking it in the present has identified elements of common ground which are often rather uninteresting simply because we can so obviously take them for granted. It is no new and enriching experience to be able to recite the Lord's Prayer or the Nicene Creed with Christians from other traditions. Instead, the richest discoveries within the ecumenical pilgrimage have been those which stand behind or indeed form the foundations of the living tradition, but which appear as distinctive elements within the living tradition and which characterise the different Christian churches throughout the world.

Equally rich, of course, has been the discovery of a deep underlying tradition which has been crystallised in the developing theology of *koinonia* or *communion*. But sometimes even a theology of communion will find it hard to embrace all of this dazzling variety which we have described. So, few would deny the Christianity alive in the Quaker tradition or within the life and work of the Salvation Army, but it would be a brave person who tried to fit either of these into the theology of communion as it has developed through the growth of ecumenical dialogue. Similarly, Sicily and England share much through their common Norman roots, but the distinctivenesses which mark off Sicilian and English religion from each other remain at least as interesting and life giving as those Romanesque arches which form the bridge of cultural unity.

Chapter 6

Patterns of Coinherence

A Glass of Vision

In the preceding chapters we have explored aspects of an evolutionary and ecological understanding of Christian doctrine, tradition, scripture interpretation and liturgy. It should, however, be clear that it belongs to the complexity of the Christian eco-system that it cannot be limited to the relatively intellectualist plane of words and ideas. So we have already touched on ways in which, for example, liturgy and typological imagery contribute to the process of Spirit-and-Tradition. Such 'ways', it should be emphasised, are not merely marginal additions to the main text of doctrine but belong to the fundamental processes by which Christian faith is communicated and, in being communicated, shaped and made what it is. As long as one remains on the intellectualist plane, however, such an ecological view is going to appear somewhat anarchic, resistant to the straitjacketing insisted on by linear and causal explanations of development. Theologians who insist too much on systematic unity or historical explanation (whether they are 'progressives' or 'conservatives') will find this unnerving – and perhaps justifiably, since such a view challenges the extent to which theology, as that has been practised in the West in recent centuries, has been too much under the sway of 'ideas men' (with the emphasis falling on *both* words). Clergy – particularly those newly released from theological college – have felt that they are failing in their duty if they are unable to give answers to those in moral perplexity or lying on their deathbeds: but this 'giving answers' is precisely a product of the intellectualist mind-set and is, in many situations, not a sign of strength or of wisdom but of insensitivity; often a shared silence or a touch of the hand would communicate far more!

What the ecological approach commits us to is to explore *everything* that might be relevant to the shape of Christian doctrine and Christian living without privileging one part of the expense of others and this means becoming sensitive to dimensions of life that have, until relatively recently, been neglected by theologians – though not, perhaps, altogether forgotten by pastors, preachers, healers, teachers of prayers and others.

Of course, it would not be difficult to argue that the last twenty years have seen the pendulum swing too far the other way – that all we hear from theologians now are calls to rehabilitate the flesh, to become aware of emotion, to affirm theological pluralism, placed there to bring into prominence all that has been suppressed by the mainstream of 'Western' thought since the triumph of ecclesiastical patriarchy. Certainly, we have no wish to declare a theological happy hour in which all manner of intoxicating beverages are purchased on the cheap and consumed at excessive speed. Nevertheless, it is begging the question (and accepting the assumptions of the intellectualist mind-set) to identify the exploration of such dimensions with a lack of discipline. On the contrary, the investigation and interpretation of that which lies outside the sphere of the word (in the narrow sense), of that which cannot be reduced to logical propositions, demands a particularly high level of discipline, even if it is a discipline which still remains to be codified and brought to the level of an objective technique.

An important example of how such an exploration can generate its own discipline and, conversely, how that discipline can lead us deeper into the theological interior has been provided by the work of Austin Farrer. Farrer will also help us to see how the process of Spirit-and-Tradition comprises elements that make for continuity without subjecting the process to the limitations of an intellectualist framework.

As we indicate later, one of the most familiar debates within Christianity is that about the place of natural and revealed theology. Often the debate has been exaggerated and polarised to suggest that the question is one of either natural theology or revealed theology. On other occasions the juxtaposition has been less severe but still one of the two has predominated. One of the reasons for this easy juxta-position has been the assumption that these two sources of theological knowledge are utterly different from each other or indeed even opposed. It was perhaps one of Austin Farrer's greatest achievements to show that the two processes need not be seen as in opposition to each other but rather complementary and effectively part of one and the same metaphysical truth. The movement of humanity and God towards each other was a unified process of revelation and rationality, of heart and mind. Through the finite, humanity is naturally drawn on to reflect upon the infinite. Much of the edifice which Farrer constructs and which brings together these two strands of theological reflection is built upon his appreciation of the place of images in Christian life, worship and discourse. This approach also allows Farrer's thought to preserve a remarkable unity binding spirituality and theology into a coherent whole. This also brought a richness to his sermons which reflected the same depths of theological insight.

The roots of this rich and integrated vision of the Christian life lie in Farrer's conviction that God and humanity, whilst separated by the necessity of the divine transcendent, never-theless are related intimately. God is the 'Creative Mind', and as such his thought wills us into existence and our actions become one with his. This does not deny our culpability, nor does it invalidate prayer, but it does set the whole universe within a single context. Humanity is involved in an act of co-creation with God; again the finite and infinite coinhere. Two quotations exemplify this trend in his thought: 'We learn ... that all finites, in being themselves and expressing their natures in their acts, are expressing also the creativity of God who creates through them.'[1] And then again, but this time in a sermon rather than part of a formal theological discourse; '... what is most freely our own is most truly God's, what is most fully our achievement is most entirely God's creation. We make ourselves what we are; but God makes us make ourselves what we are.'[2] The natural and the supernatural are thus to be seen as a continuum, and the ulti-mate exemplification of this for Farrer is, of course, in the incarnation of God in Jesus Christ. This unified theological vision requires that prayer and doctrine, rational and ascetic theology, never be separated. Christian thought, prayer and sacrament together reflect the co-creative life of humanity in God.

The effect of this unified vision also allowed Farrer to contribute with great originality to a variety of different theological disciplines. He expounded a developed philosophical Thomism, rooted in the thought of Thomas Aquinas, but expressed in concepts which take into account contemporary developments. He produced a number of volumes of a literary-critical nature within the discipline of New Testament theology. Again the influence of images is powerful and his biblical theology is most effective when he is dealing with authors who themselves are rich in figurative language; so, for example, his two books on the Revelation of St John the Divine are particularly convincing in their argument.[3] He also wrote on theodicy[4], and finally he was a noted preacher and writer on prayer.

The single most dominant influence on Farrer, his theology and spirituality, as seen through his sermons and as glimpsed through his speculative theology, was then that of figural imagination. He poured out images both in his homiletic style and in his written prose. His use of images and the key part which he sees images playing in the development of the tradition testify to this: 'The human imagination has always been controlled by certain basic images, in which man's own nature, his relation to his fellows, and his dependence upon the divine power find expression.'[5] Farrer follows most often, in his work, the Western 'way of affirmation of images'. His perennial concern for analogy and imagery mirror this fact. The Eastern Dionysian 'way of negation' breaks through on occasions and most clearly when he is describing the role of analogy and imagery in Christian theology and revelation: '...images are crucified by the reality, slowly and progressively, never completely, and not always without pain: yet the reality is better than the images. Jesus Christ clothed himself in all the images of messianic promise, and in living them out crucified them: but the crucified reality is better than the figures of prophecy.'[6]

For Farrer, imagery is essential and irreducible, but it is not final. The supernatural act in humanity is a foretaste, and only a foretaste, of the whole substance of the saving mystery and the *final* fusion of humanity in God.

Farrer may well have developed his theory of images in the exchange of ideas between himself and his friend Charles Williams. Williams and Farrer also shared an appreciation for the language of 'coinherence'. In Williams, the term is used specifically. In Farrer, the theme is basic to much of his work, both in his sermons and in his speculative theology of creation and divine providence. The term derives from the writings of early Christianity, notably the Cappadocian Fathers and is synonymous with the Greek term 'perichoresis'. It implies the mutual pervasion of God and humanity. Charles Williams puts it thus: 'Coinherence had been the very pattern of Christendom; we were not to be merely inheritors but "brethren and fellows and coinheritors of the name of salvation".'

Coinherence, as a ground bass to much of his thought, was useful to Farrer in developing his theology and spirituality, rooted as it was in images as the means of exchange, participation, and the union of humanity and God. As a model it speaks to both spiritual growth and theological interpretation. It identifies an acute appreciation of the living tradition. It speaks doctrinally of the relationship between God and humanity and here once again the mutual interests of Williams and Farrer become very clear. Williams writes: 'From childbirth to the Divine Trinity Itself the single nature thrives; there is here no difference between that *natural* and that *supernatural*'.[7]

The most original of Farrer's writings was perhaps his Bampton Lectures, *The Glass of Vision*, in which he attempted to expound a theory of biblical inspiration. It is here that he brought together the traditions of natural and revealed theology in a particularly creative manner. In this book he reflected a similar pattern of thought to that which we have just quoted from Charles Williams. The natural/supernatural overlap is central to his argument. Indeed, it is through images once again that the human mind may leap up to perform a supernatural act. This Farrer picks up in his reflections on the Eucharist and he writes at one point: 'The natural and the supernatural joined when Christ was conceived in Mary by the Holy Ghost. The mystery is continued and extended in this Holy Sacrament.'[8] Coinherence, then, as a concept lying behind Farrer's thought is important since it acts as one of the springs from which both the unity of his theology and spirituality and the centring on images flows.

Coinherence and the possibility of humanity co-operating with God is Farrer's starting point for prayer. He writes: 'Prayer is the practical expression from our side of the conviction that the Creator works by making his creatures make themselves.' Further on he reflects: 'When [Christ] talked about prayer he talked from within the enterprise on which he and his disciples were engaged. God would achieve the salvation of his people through the instruments he had chosen, if those instruments lent themselves to his purpose.'[9] Prayer is thus crucially concerned with the seeking of the divine will and co-operating with it. This is developed with some sophistication in regard to theology and revelation in his Bampton Lectures. Here he sets out a framework on which to hang theology and spirituality by concerning himself with how we appropriate the form of divine truth through our own reason. These lectures thus form the nexus of Farrer's theological reasoning, relating revelation, natural theology and spirituality within one total matrix.

He begins by discussing the relationship of the natural to the supernatural. The key is that the natural and the supernatural overlap and that one may act as the gateway to the other. The universal truth of God may be appreciated through the contingency of the particular realities of the natural world and our experience of it. Farrer rejects the suggestion that we meet God through a supernatural effect upon the mind; he prefers instead the notion of the natural and supernatural as a clear continuum. God is pictured as always permeating the human mind: 'I would dare to think that sometimes my thought would become diaphanous, so that there should be some perception of the divine cause shining through the created effect, as a deep pool, settling into a clear tranquility, permits us to see the spring in the bottom of it from which its waters rise.'[10]

The analogy of the pool is a useful figure for comprehending his understanding of the divine and how we may come to God through our appreciation of images. Farrer's point is that God is there present in us. It is for us to identify his presence, and the incarnation is central to this process. It is through Jesus that the coinherence of God and humanity has been made explicit. Bare theism without the person of Jesus is insufficient. Christ is thus both the key to our finding God and the type whom we must follow.

This merging of the natural and supernatural as we seek God through our minds is further explained by Farrer as mutual interpenetration. He points to the danger in seeing supernatural acts as merely those inexplicable in natural terms. This is only one step away from ascribing superstitious happenings to the divine. Instead we aspire to the supernatural ourselves, rising out of our dependence and permeating his mind, as we transcend ourselves and partake of his supernaturality.[11] This will be the natural inclination as the human mind contemplates the divine, as that mind aligns itself with God. It is the destination to which we gaze and we attempt to 'see' the world in the context of the divine.[12] Thus the supernatural act is continuous with natural human activity, but is it not then merely natural? No, argues Farrer. The finite does indeed exclude the finite, but the infinite is not excluded. We may act as God's co-creators. We do not aspire to total infinitude or indeed we should be asserting our full divinity. Rather, we tend in the direction of the infinite, and there is thus no discontinuity when we achieve the supernatural act.

Farrer goes on to ask exactly where images and inspiration fit into this plan, both in Holy Scripture and elsewhere. In Scripture, he argues, they are not divinely dictated, but are rather the reactions to circumstances and feelings. Jesus Christ is the primary revelation, the height of supernaturality, where first and second causes perfectly unite, to put it in Aristotelian terms. Images both in the Bible and outside play upon our minds to reveal the divine to us. Divine truth, then, is supernaturally communicated to humanity in an act of inspired thinking, which falls into the shape of certain images, but how do such images signify divine realities? [13] The answer is not obvious; indeed, this raises in the doctrine of analogy one of the central problems of metaphysics. Farrer points to the commonplaces of this doctrine. Metaphysics is seen as the description of natural mysteries by the critique of analogies.[14] Models including either too many positive or too many negative analogies become eroded of meaning.

From this, it follows that theology is the elaborated form of thinking of the believing Christian, and so metaphysics is the elaborated form of contemplation. It also follows that by means of images and analogies we are led to understand natural mysteries. We are brought to discourse about God through the 'shadow of God in finite being'.[15] The finite manifests itself as the shadow of the infinite – there is almost a Platonic feel about this. One of the chief ways by which this manifestation occurs is by means of 'archetype'. These archetypes, based perhaps on family or kinship, are primary sources of imagery, but not exclusive; rather God is revealed by all. Farrer argues that such archetypes are useful in their universality. Such images are inspired; they arise and form when we aspire to the supernatural act. Scripture may, in one sense, be approached as a universal dictionary – or, perhaps better, a universal grammar – of such archetypes.

Farrer goes on to review the use of images in the form of poetry. He compares the poet with the prophet. The poet is bound by no conventions or restrictions, as was the prophet by the presuppositions and beliefs of Jewish ethical monotheism, although the two have a certain amount in common: 'What the prophet shares with the latter day poet then, is the technique of inspiration chiefly; both move on incantation of images under a control.'[16] A similar argument is stated for the poetry of the New Testament. This then is the connecting link between the biblical image and the image used by the poet. The poet still speaks to human religious sensibilities. Even contemporary humanity, given the ability to 'see', may derive from all around an inspiration which guides us to the divine. Hence, using the medium of poetry alongside the tool of critical analogy, imagery is not invalidated as a contemporary road towards the divine. The divine and human are seen to be reaching out toward one another.

Of course, Farrer would talk of the ultimate mystery of God's communication with humanity. Nothing is final; images must be crucified. We can only gaze into the dark pool, and hence we shall never see God on this earth with complete clarity. The glass of vision into which we gaze is still that of St Paul, through which we see only darkly. The emphasis is clear in Farrer's fond quotation of two favourite New Testament passages: 'It does not yet appear what we shall be' (1 John 3.2) and 'What no eye has seen, no ear heard, nor the heart of man conceived, what God has prepared for those who love Him' (1 Cor. 2.9 cf. Isaiah 64.4). To pick another of his favourite images, we can only work and pray for the 'mind of Christ' that we may move nearer to God.

This whole issue, then, of the place of images lies behind his biblical scholarship. Whilst as we have hinted, he used some of the tools of biblical criticism, he attacked the form critics and what he felt was the strait-jacket which they placed around various biblical writers and their books. In some ways he pre-empted much redaction criticism in calling for the writers to be allowed to speak their own theology. Similar concerns permeate his preaching, and throughout images are used with such skill that it is hard to discern where one has moved on from the illustration to the theological reflection into which the sermon is taking us. His best sermons are perfectly flowing works of art, often beginning with an image set in the 'every day' and leading by means of an expository section to the transcendent reality of God. Even the Trinitarian doxology is no afterthought; it is woven into the sermon and is one of the means of leaving his congregation in heaven as well as on earth.

To conclude these reflections with reference again to Farrer's preaching is appropriate in the context of our wider discussion of the spirit and the living tradition. Farrer's use of poetry is not simply technique, but rather underpins his entire understanding of theology and the means whereby humanity is capable of appreciating the activity and nature of God. Others too have reflected upon the parallels between preaching and poetry, which is rooted in the significance of images for Christian theology. So R. E. C. Browne: 'The Christian religion can never be presented without imagery. Exact prose could not replace the allusiveness that makes imagery the only precision in proclaiming the gospel ... What is true of poetry is also true of preaching: the great sermon presents the Gospel images in a way that does not startle but which commands attention. The preacher often begins work on his sermon not by constructing an abstract statement but by reflecting on an image and letting it drop in his mind as it gives rise to image after image in a connection which is not fortuitous but according to the laws of images.'[17]

Ideas and Angels

Farrer speaks of archetypes that appear in the images of prophetic and apostolic poetry and that combine in themselves both 'finite' and 'infinite', both 'human' and 'divine' aspects. To become aware of these archetypes we need – minimally – the kind of sensibility that we bring to our best reading of the best poetry. Such awareness is illumined by a more-than-rational light that, instead of trying to get 'behind' the images to what they mean, finds the images themselves charged with communicative power.

Yet if Farrer helps us to get beyond an excessively verbalised and intellectualised way of doing theology, his concept of archetypes could be read as implying an exclusivism that would limit the archetypes to the very specific history of revelation enshrined in the Judaeo-Christian scriptures. Is the power and manner of working of such archetypes something completely unparalleled? Or do they build on and interact with archetypal structures operative elsewhere in human life?

To speak of archetypes in the twentieth century is, almost inevitably, to speak of the Swiss psychologist Carl Gustav Jung, for the theory of archetypes was one of the cornerstones of Jung's thought and one of the areas in which he has had an extensive influence on wide areas of cultural life. Jung's sympathetic approach to religion has led to frequent and important dialogues between Jungians and representatives of many faiths. Although some of his ideas have a more immediate connection with Eastern religious traditions (as in his frequent allusions to the Eastern figure of the mandala) there are also significant points of contact with Christianity, both in terms of the detailed study of particular images and archetypes and, more profoundly, in terms of the overall structure of his thought. It is important to say, however, that, much as he valued religious experience, Jung did not claim to be a believer in anything like the conventional sense and in using his thought at this point we do not claim that his thought is 'Christian'. Instead we focus upon its value to Christians in examining the processes by which Christian experience, Christian symbols and Christian truths are communicated.

Before turning directly to Jung, however, we shall look briefly at another writer, Charles Williams, whose own theory of archetypes, or, more precisely of an archetypal order underlying and informing the world, provides a kind of bridge between the (perhaps) more exclusively Christian vision of Farrer and the effectively universal syncretism of Jung.

Williams was, arguably, one of the most singular of twentieth century English writers. A reader for the Oxford University Press, a friend and associate not only of Farrer but of C. S. Lewis, his religious vision reflects an enormous reading of both theology and general literature, with Dante, Shakespeare and the Arthurian legends each playing an important role, yet – for both good and ill – without the particular discipline and colouring of an academic training in theology.

As well as such theoretical works as *The Image of the City* he also produced a series of what have been described as 'supernatural thrillers' in which his philosophy of the coinherence of worlds was given dramatic form. As works of literature they probably do not rank much higher than Agatha Christie. Indeed, there is more than a passing similarity to the 'Queen of Crime' in that these novels are typically set in a very ordinary pre-war English town or village and the characters are drawn from the same range of

English 'types' that we might expect to find in one of Miss Christie's weekend house parties. As in a Miss Marple tale we then discover that all is not what it seems and that behind this ordinary, comfortable façade a whole other world of motivation and passion is concealed. There, however, the similarity ends, for whereas the detective story deals in wills, secret criminal pasts, torrid love affairs and so on, the 'hidden' world revealed in a Williams' novel is one of moral and spiritual warfare. Let us take an example.

The Place of the Lion opens with the friends Anthony Durrant and Quentin Sabot walking down a lane in rural Hertfordshire on a long summer evening. What could be safer – except, as the friends soon discover, that a lioness has escaped from a travelling circus and is on the loose. Unfortunately for them it is not long before they run into her, or, rather see her as they shelter in the porch of an empty house. Following a scene of confusion in which – apparently – the lioness springs upon a man they have seen approaching the house, the moonlight shadows clear and they see, not the lioness but

> ... the shape of a full-grown and tremendous lion, its head flung back, its mouth open, its body quivering. It ceased to roar and gathered itself back into itself. It was a lion such as the young men had never seen in any zoo or menagerie; it was gigantic and seemed to their dazed senses to be growing larger every moment.[18]

How, they ask each other, could a lioness have turned into a lion? What did they really see? What really happened? – But this is only the beginning of a series of peculiar events. Mr Tighe, father of Damaris (with whom Anthony is in love), has a passion for lepidoptery and, a few days after the encounter with the lion, Anthony comes across him leaning over the gate of the house where the lion manifestation had taken place. Their conversion is suddenly interrupted by the appearance of an extraordinary butterfly:

> It was a terrific, colossal butterfly, it looked as if it were two feet or more across from wing-tip to wing-tip. It was tinted and coloured with every conceivable brightness; green and orange predominating. It was moving upward in spiral flutterings, upward to a certain point, from which it seemed directly to fall

close to the ground, then again it began its upward sweep, and again hovered and fell ...lovely and self-sufficient it went on with its complex manoeuvres in the air.

Then an even more extraordinary sight meets their eyes.

> [Anthony] looked back at the marvel in time to see, from somewhere above his own head, another brilliancy – but much smaller – flash through the air, almost as if some ordinary butterfly had hurtled itself towards its more gigantic image. And another followed it, and another, and as Anthony, now thoroughly roused, sprang up and aside, to see the better, he beheld the air full of them. Those of which he had caught sight were but the scattered first comers of a streaming host. Away across the fields they came, here in thick masses, there in thinner lines, white and yellow, green and red, purple and blue and dusky black. They were sweeping round, in great curving flights; mass following after mass, he saw them driving forward from far away, but not directly, taking wide distances in their sweep, now on one side, now on another, but always and all of them speeding forward towards the gate and the garden beyond.
>
> (PL, pp. 40–1)

Once arrived in the garden this great multitude of butterflies seems somehow, magically, to be absorbed into the single great butterfly that Tighe and Anthony had first seen. Tighe, whose lifelong passion we may recall, has been lepidoptery, is speechless with wonder. ' " O that I should see it!" he said again. "O glory be to it!" He wiped away his tears with his knuckles, and looked back at the garden. "O the blessed sight," he went on. "And I saw it. O what have I done to deserve it?" ' (PL, p. 43)

The explanation for these astonishing sightings of supernatural lions and butterflies is that, through the magical experiments of Berringer, the owner of the house where the manifestations take place, those powers which the ancient world knew as Platonic ideas and which the Middle Ages knew as angelic orders have been released into the world. As they become manifest they draw to themselves those creatures whose essential 'idea' they are. Thus, individuals – such as the lioness or the multitude of English butterflies that come flooding across the fields – are reabsorbed into their archetypal idea, under the form of the Lion or the Butterfly. But these forms themselves are only images for moral or spiritual values, the Lion for strength and dominion, the Butterfly for beauty. Human beings too come to reveal their true archetypal character, manifesting the form of the idea that they have – consciously or unconsciously – served all their lives. So, the seemingly insipid Miss Wilmot, an attender at Berringer's occult discussion group, turns out to be the author of a series of poison-pen letters, twisted by envy and malice – what Nietzsche described as *ressentiment*. Before the shocked eyes of Richardson, the bookseller's assistant, who is also a member of the group, she reveals here true form:

> Her body was writing into curves and knots where she lay, as if cramps convulsed her. Her mouth was open but she could not scream: her hands were clutching at her twisted throat. In her wide eyes there was now no malice, only an agony, and gradually all her body and head were drawn up backwards from the floor by an invisible force, so that from the hips she remained rigidly upright and her legs lay stretched straight out behind her upon the ground, as if a serpent in human shape raised itself before him. (PL, p. 151)

By the end of the scene the transformation is complete. Through the subserviency of Miss Wilmot the dark angelic energy of the serpent has found shape and is let loose in the world.

Williams' argument in *The Place of the Lion* is not that such powers are inherently evil but that they become evil when they are not subject to the hierarchical order of the divine scheme of things. When that order is broken, then even 'good' powers such as the regal strength of the Lion or the beauty of the Butterfly become all-consuming and potentially destructive. In the novel it is through Anthony Durrant's identification with the Eagle, the power of true knowledge, then the rebel powers, set loose by the self-seeking dabbling of Berringer and his disciples, are once more brought into order and the world returns to 'normal'. Only, of course, we now know that 'normal' reality is not so normal and that even the apparently trivial affairs of ordinary people in comfortable rural England are at all times expressive of a commitment to moral and spiritual values of one or other kind. Spiritual warfare and the striving for a proper ordering of the archetypal world is the true sub-text of 'everyday life'.

If all this sounds more than a little bizarre (as it is), it is nevertheless clear that the underlying symbolism of the novel is drawn from familiar Christian and biblical sources, coupled (as Christianity has been coupled for nearly two millennia!) with a somewhat adapted form of Platonism. These Christian sources become clear when, in the chapter 'The Naming of the Beasts', Damaris sees Anthony as the new Adam, reversing the drama of Eden and regaining paradise – or at least its possibility.

> ... she looked again upon the glade of the garden where the image of Adam named the beasts, and naming ruled them. But now he was farther from her, nearer to those twin mysterious trees in the centre. Among the shapes that pressed about him she could not at first well discern one from another, but as she leaned and strained to see she beheld them gathering into two companies. There fell over the whole scene a strange and lovely clearness, shed from the wings of a soaring wonder that ... flew, scattering light. The intermingled foliage of the trees of knowledge and of life – if indeed they were separate – received it; amid those branches the eagle which was the living act of science sank and rested. But far below the human figure stood and on either side of it were the shapes of the lion and the lamb. His hand rested on the head of the one; the other paused by him. In and for that exalted moment all acts of peace that then had being through the world were deepened and knew their own nature more clearly ... Friendships grew closer; intentions of love possessed their right fulfilment. Terrors of malice and envy and jealousy faded; disordered beauty everywhere recognized the sacred laws that governed it. Man dreamed of himself in the place of his creation. (PL, pp. 203–4)

All this is seen by Damaris 'as Eve might have watched the movements of her companion'. (There is no doubt that Williams made assumptions about gender that could not pass without question today – although in another novel he does introduce a female Messiah-figure.)

Williams, then, is saying that, despite all appearances, whether of English comfortableness or of supposed modernity, the Christian 'myth' or the Christian archetypal order still has the potential not merely to explain but actively to

order and to transform contemporary reality. Without necessarily accepting the angelic schema he offers in *The Place of
the Lion*, we may take his fictionalised speculations as one
way of conceiving how the biblical archetypes mooted by
Farrer take shape and are active in the world of social and
personal relationships. It is, once more, the pattern of coinherence, of the divine and the human worlds constantly
interacting and interdependent.

This pattern also helps us to think further the relationship
between continuity and change in the tradition. The notion
of an archetypal order, underlying and sustaining the world
of appearances, can, in the form Williams gives it, allow for
a constant reshaping of the external appearances whilst
asserting a fundamental identity with certain perennial principles and values. Far from it being the case that such an
'idealist' view inhibits change and development, it is part of
the proper working of the ideas that they generate constantly
new shapes and forms. It is only when their true order is
disordered – as, in *The Place of the Lion*, they are disordered
by the spiritual ambition of Berringer – that the 'ideas' end
up by consuming the reality of everyday life with all its flux
and change. Their real task is precisely to facilitate the
unfolding of creation in all its variety, in all its plenitude and
richness of being.

Interestingly, Williams also explores how non-Christian
schemes of symbolism can be correlated with the Christian
archetypal order, as he conceives it. *In The Greater Trumps*,
for instance, a sequence of archetypal manifestations takes
place, not dissimilar to that described in *The Place of the
Lion*. This time, however, the structure is provided, not by
Platonic ideas nor by medieval angelology, but, by the
'Greater Trumps' of the Tarot. This may sound dangerously
'New Age' to some, but the key to the proper ordering of the
Tarot symbolism is again located in a thoroughly Christian
context – only this time it is in the Incarnation (the story
takes place at Christmas time) that provides the theological
resolution, rather than (as in *The Place of the Lion*) the
creation narrative. Tellingly, one of the principal characters is
called 'Sybil', the name of an apocryphal prophecy fore-
telling the advent of the Messiah – a clue that the relationship

between the Tarot and Christianity is being conceived on the model of Old/New Testament, of prophecy and fulfilment. In other words, William is saying that all symbolic schemes ultimately connect with and are explicable in terms of the Christian scheme. The point, however, is not thereby to devalue such schemes but to show their metaphysical convergence with Christianity. The parallels with Farrer are striking, the theme of coinherence being of particular importance.

This pattern of coinherence, or of identity-in-difference as we may call it, recurs throughout Williams' work. For Williams the doctrine is summed up in a phrase he cites on a number of occasions, a phrase taken from an unidentified mystical source: 'This also is Thou; neither is this Thou.' That is to say, God's relation to the world is one that is at all times and in all places a relation of identity *and* of difference. Everything is both natural *and* supernatural. Divine truth is to be found in all things and in all human seekings after truth – yet none ever completely grasp or perfectly express the divine truth itself. It is, at every point, a case of 'in a glass darkly' – yet even such darkened vision is nonetheless vision of a sort.

Archetypes and the Self

We have been seeing how, in the writings of Austin Farrer and of Charles Williams, a theory of Christian archetypes does three things. Firstly, it provides the assurance of continuity in the face of what otherwise might seem to be a totally disorientating vision of ceaseless change. Secondly, it provides a way of speaking about the coinherence, the identity-in-difference, that characterizes the relationship between creator and created, infinite and finite being. Thirdly, it calls for qualities of discernment and of sensibility that go far beyond the narrow intellectualism and overemphasis on conscious, verbalized knowledge that has dominated much of the recent Christian tradition. To live with knowledge of the archetypes is to be able to see past the superficial conscious and deliberate self-representations of things and persons. We are now seeing that, in awakening such sensibilities, a theory of archetypal forms also involves appealing to patterns of thinking, of imagination and of feeling that are universal – albeit in many diverse and strange guises – amongst human beings. To explore further how such a pre-programming of human consciousness that makes it receptive to the Gospel images might be envisaged, we now turn to the work of C. G. Jung, one of the twentieth century's most influential if also controversial, thinkers.

The theory of archetypes is one of the main buttresses of Jung's psychology. It is important, however, to remember that Jung was first and foremost a practising analyst and that his theories were shaped by the therapeutic processes he experienced with his patients. Like Freud he worked primarily through the data provided by patients' dreams and, again like Freud, he believed that dreams disclosed attitudes, wishes and fears, repressed by the conscious mind. But whereas Freud believed that these unconscious forces were all ultimately explicable in terms of sexuality, Jung believed that, if anything, the sexual itself was ultimately symbolic of a deeper reality that he understood as 'spiritual'.

Every human being, according to Jung, is engaged in a process which he called the 'process of individuation'. This process has been described by M.-L. von Franz in the following terms as:

> ... a meandering pattern in which individual strands or tenden-cies become visible, then vanish, then return again. If one watches this meandering design over a long period of time, one can observe a sort of hidden regulating or directing tendency at work, creating a slow, imperceptible process of psychic growth ... Gradually a wider and more mature personality emerges, and by degrees becomes effective and even visible to others ... this psychic growth ... cannot be brought about by a conscious effort of will power, but happens involuntarily and naturally, [and] it is in dreams frequently symbolized by the tree, whose slow, powerful, involuntary growth fulfills a definite pattern.[19]

We are, that is to say, so structured that, from the very beginning of our lives, we are in search of a stable and abiding identity and, to the extent that we find such an identity, such a self, we also have a psychic structure designed to preserve and sustain that self, ensuring constancy and stability. Thus, when the circumstances of our lives – whether it is the general, alienated and alienating rush of twentieth century urban living, or whether it is our response to a particular personal crisis – lead to our losing the thread of psychic growth or stability (being untrue to our selves), then the psyche has mechanisms by which to lead us back to the path of authentic selfhood. Among these mechanisms are the archetypcal figures revealed in dreams. These are best explained by means of an example – and perhaps one of the most significant examples Jung himself gives is that of the 'anima' or feminine principle.

Jung regards the whole human being as essentially balanced, with heart and head, feeling and intellect each needing to be represented. Similarly – indeed, especially – this same pattern of balance applies to the masculine and feminine principles. Each of us needs a sensitive awareness of and responsiveness to the opposite sex. No one is 'all man' without any admixture of the feminine nor 'all woman' without any admixture of the male! Thus, if an individual, because of social or family pressures, comes to act out exaggerated male roles and suppresses the values associated in his society with women, he will, clearly, be a one-sided individual. In a Jungian perspective, at least, this is unhealthy and inherently unstable. The dreams of such an individual will probably compensate for this imbalance by producing images associated with feminine values that the dreamer is being called upon by the depth-structure of his psyche to recognise and to accept. Such images will be supremely focused in the 'anima', the feminine counter-image that compensates for the individual's conscious masculinity. In the sphere of religion devotion to female deities – Jung would say that Mary has this function in some Christian traditions – reflects a similar need at a public, social level.

Another important archetype is that of the mandala. This is a figurative form, widely used as a focus for meditation in Buddhism, in which a sequence of concentric (usually) circular shapes lead the eye towards the representation of the deity at the centre. For Jung, this use of the mandala is symbolic of the quest for the self that underlies our whole psychic life. Although formalised in Buddhism he found many other examples of such shapes in the art of many different cultures, in the ground-plan of significant religious sites and, not least, in spontaneous paintings produced by patients. He noticed, however, that in much modern art and in the mandalas painted by his patients, the space at the centre which would usually be filled by the deity was empty. He took this to mean that whereas a traditional religion such as Buddhism provided individuals with a ready-made structure in and through which to find their true selves, the situation of modernity was such that individuals were left adrift without any clear prototype, without any ultimate role model, left to do the work of individuation on their own and in their own way.

Potentially the whole of human culture becomes comprehensible, on the Jungian view, as an accumulated sequence of expressions of this psychic quest for selfhood or wholeness. Fairy tales, art and architecture, political movements and their myths – even such modern myths as that of scientific progress – are all examined in these terms. This, for example, is how M.-L. von Franz describes the 1953 French Film *Crin Blanc*:

> Wild horses often symbolize the uncontrollable instinctive drives that can erupt from the unconscious – and that many people try to repress. In the film, the horse and a boy form a strong attachment (though the horse still runs wild with his herd). But local horsemen set out to capture the wild horses. The stallion and his boy rider are pursued for miles; finally they are cornered on the seashore. Rather than submit to capture, the boy and the horse plunge into the sea to be swept away. Symbolically, the story's end seems to represent an escape into the unconscious (the sea) as a way to avoid facing reality in the outside world.[20]

The material that Jungians analyse in this way is thus enormously varied, indeed, co-extensive with all the images and texts that human beings produce – although Jung always had a particularly strong interest in religious myths and images as providing the clearest and most forceful examples of archetypal symbolism. In religion the archetypes that inform and shape cultural images are presented in, as it were, a pure form. These archetypes, Jung believed, were universal, belonging to the inheritance of every human being – he often spoke of what he called 'the collective unconscious' – or, at least, of particular cultural groups. As the example of *Crin Blanc* also makes clear the presence of archetypes gives a peculiar intensity to experience: the kind of intensity that is to be found in poetry and art, when we fall in love or in the presence of death.

There has, inevitably, been much debate as to how far Jung's way of thinking can be squared with orthodox Christianity. Certainly there are more obvious links with aspects of Eastern religions and, as we have noted there is little to suggest that Jung himself (a pastor's son) was a believer in any conventional sense. His fascination with matters religious and theological was first and foremost to do with their psychological interest and value. But, even if we have reservations about aspects of 'Jungianism', his theory helps us in several ways. First of all, it indicates how many diverse cultural forms and images can be understood through certain fundamental 'types'. At the same time, these 'types' do not limit or constrain the creation and expression of images and symbols – on the contrary they are always fruitful and multiplying. It is striking, in this respect, that when, for example, Jung speaks of the empty space at the centre of many modern mandalas he is showing how old archetypes can be modified or newly represented in the light of new experiences – or even how new archetypes can rise. Understanding the world through archetypes does not mean subordinating the richness of an ever-evolving reality to a rigid, limited and static schema. It is not simply a matter of 'explaining', but, in the spirit of ecology, of looking at the whole picture – 'The truth is the whole' – to which both divine and human, finite and infinite contribute.

But, secondly, this not only provides a parallel to the way in which certain fundamental symbols continue to inform the extraordinary diversity of Christian traditions. It also shows how we might think of humanity's psychic life as being naturally and inherently oriented towards such symbols; how, as it were, the natural mental life of human beings is shaped by a symbolic structure that has a 'natural affinity' towards the specific symbolic structure of Christianity; or, we might say, the attraction is mutual! (Here Williams' model of biblical narratives fulfilling the Platonic or Romany symbolic systems is relevant.)

Lastly, we are once again warned off attempting to understand the kind of coherence that characterises religion exclusively in terms of intellectual or verbal formulations. Religion speaks to us in many and diverse media, old and new. It is never just a matter of words.

Chapter 7

Beyond Words

Theological Art

Our argument has suggested at many points that the materials and the forms of the process of Spirit-and-Tradition cannot be limited to that which can be grasped on the intellectual plane or to that which can be expressed in verbal formulae. The roots of religious thinking, behaving and communicating plunge deep into the human psyche, into the sphere of those archetypal forms and patterns that shape our experience before and beyond words. As bearers of the tradition we find ourselves both receiving and giving out far more than we are ever consciously aware of at any one time. Nor is this simply a matter of acquiring a kind of artistic skill in dealing with images and symbols – something we might learn as we learn a craft (though that is, arguably, no worse a model than the model of the academy!). It is already at work in our fundamental body-language, the very gestures we use and the way we use them.

Some traditions within the Church have been aware of this in at least a subliminal way. Think, for a moment, of the 'language' involved in posture when we pray or engage in liturgy. The Eastern Church has, for instance, always insisted on the faithful standing for prayers during the period from Easter to Ascension – and, after many generations in which the ministerial 'Let us pray' has been heard as 'Let us kneel', many Anglicans have been rediscovering the symbolic value of a standing posture during prayer. At the same time it would be tragic if the no less powerful symbolism of kneeling were to be altogether lost – though kneeling itself has many variants, each of which gives expression to a particular aspect of the prayer-relationship. There is also, as La Rochefoucauld noted, an eloquence which consists in the tone and inflection of the voice as much as in the choice of words, and it is no secret that particular religious traditions have institutionalised particular mannerisms of speech. Although this is superficially doing no more than making things easy for the Church's comic impersonators, it may be that there are particular patterns and rhythms of speech that, in certain situations, facilitate the work of Christian communication. We might, for instance, think of what is implied in saying of a pastor that he or she has 'a good bedside manner', a knack, as it seems, of establishing instant communication even with a previously unknown sufferer who is, perhaps, in a state of diminished and fading consciousness anyway.

Nonetheless, in emphasising the intuitive and sublimal nature of certain dimensions of Spirit-and-Tradition (what the Orthodox theologian Vladimir Lossky has called 'the margin of silence' that accompanies all words of revelation)[1], it is not quite the case that, in Wittgenstein's phrase: 'of that whereof we cannot speak we must keep silent'. There are dimensions of the communication process that do give themselves to be thought, even though they cannot be coralled by any rationalistic system of classification. It is in our experience of art and in the role of art in the tradition that we find the easiest point of access to such dimensions. In this chapter, therefore, we shall look at three areas in which such experience makes its presence felt in the process of Spirit-and-Tradition, using examples that help us to reflect on our contemporary experience of image, of architecture and of music, three media by which the Church takes shape in the world and communicates itself to the world *yet very often without being aware of so doing*! We aim, then, to undertake an exercise in 'theological art', not as aiming to say all that could be said, but simply as a means of drawing attention to this much neglected but powerful area.

A Journey and an Image

In the summer of 1990 Lincoln Cathedral became the focus of a new kind of pilgrimage, a pilgrimage that drew together artists and critics, believers and those in search of belief and the simply curious, united in what the organizers called 'The

Journey'. 'The Journey' was, at the factual level, a visual arts project organized by the city's Usher Gallery and involving a number of artists in creating specially commissioned works at sites in and around Lincoln, all centred on the Cathedral itself. At the same time the gallery provided resources for visitors to learn about the different journeys and the aims of the artists involved as well as a separate exhibition of 'New Icons', works of contemporary art which had a direct religious reference.

The works created for 'The Journey' were not, mostly, of an obvious or overt religious kind. Roger Ackling, for instance, created a series of works made by using a magnifying glass to burn geometrical patterns on pieces of driftwood, works which had something of the archaic quality of primitive ritual art. Eileen Lawrence, using an idea from the Buddhist tradition, made a sequence of 'prayer sticks', thin strips of watercoloured paper, designed for and hung in the circular Chapter House to enhance the invitation to prayer and meditation offered by that space. Jennifer Durrant, an abstract artist, painted two large works to be installed beneath the east windows of the north and south aisles of the Cathedral, works which reacted to her experience of the atmosphere and colour of the two aisles. Another site specific installation in the Cathedral was a photographic work by Gary Fabian Miller, an extraordinarily concentrated image of light irradiating a blade of grass. In a quite different mode, one of the younger contributors, Sue Hilder, used organic, vegetable materials – reeds, spines, etc. – found at Tupholme Abbey, a ruined site some miles outside Lincoln, to lure and provoke visitors into a new experience of the site and its surroundings.

The best-known contributor was, perhaps, Craigie Aitchison, one of whose many paintings of the crucifixion was shown in the Church of St Mary Magdalene in Lincoln. These paintings reduce the scene to a bare minimum. Against a background of powerfully dominant colour, sometimes recalling the hills of his Scottish upbringing, the cross itself is stripped down to a pole and the Christ figure often appears – at least at first glance – as armless, or as if his arms are tied behind the upright stake of the cross. The most controversial exhibit, however, was Leonard McComb's polished bronze figure 'Portrait of Young Man Standing', soon familiar as 'The Golden Man' and much-discussed in the national press as, on account of its nudity, it was moved from site to site within the Cathedral before passing to a more receptive home in the Tate Gallery.

The works were, therefore, quite disparate, both in style and in content. The contributors could not be said in any way to form a school or movement. There was, perhaps, a common concern to re-root human experience in nature, to look to organic form and to allow organic materials and processes to play a part in the artistic process, thus getting away from renaissance and romantic ideals of the artist as an almost godlike creator, producing work more or less in a vacuum or subjecting the material to his shaping will. In the words of Sue Hilder: 'The Journey through the land is a way of discovery and re-discovery. The traveller does not impose but absorbs and reacts intuitively, discovering forms and processes of balance in nature, and re-discovering innate spiritual balance ... My journey through the land is a series of moments when human nature and land nature come together. These moments are windows of perception.'[2]

Such a concern for finding in nature the clue to linking art and the spiritual is well-precedented in the history of theological reflection on art. There are perhaps many who would share the conviction of the theologian Jacques Maritain that the builders of Lincoln Cathedral, for example, achieved what they did because they had a sense for 'the logic of the structure of the living thing, and [of] the intimate geometry of nature', a logic that made what they built 'eternally mysterious and disturbing'.[3] They had, in the wonderful phrase of Umberto Eco, commenting on the medieval theory of art, a vision of the 'structural grace in things'.[4] Closer to home, Ruskin too made the spiritual value of natural forms central to his understanding of art, seeing the natural creation as a complex network of 'types' of divine values such as beauty, unity, purity and justice. Creation, he believed, was ordered to serve the education of humanity – not that nature was sufficient to lead us to a personal relationship with God, but that it was one preliminary step in that direction.

There is, of course, always room for debate as to how well an exhibition (or, better, event) such as 'The Journey' fulfils its stated aims. The controversial critic, Peter Fuller, wrote of Richard Long, whose work was exhibited in the Cathedral in the course of 'The Journey', that it 'is symptomatic of *the loss* [our emphasis] of both the aesthetic and the spiritual dimensions of art; he shows little trace of imagination, of skill, of the transformation of materials ... His work is sentimental and fetishistic.'[5] The piece in question, 'Halifax Circle', consisted of a number of rough pieces of Cornish slate, arranged in a solid circle and set in the south transept of the Cathedral, almost like a segment of rough-and-ready landscape. Don Cupitt, on the other hand, finds in such works of Long's a powerful expression of sacredness, communicated by 'their austerity and impersonality, and by their matter-of-fact acceptance of their own transience. They seem to speak to us of an enduring unnameable Background against which our brief life is acted out ... It may be a starting-point for the religion of the future.'[6]

Art (or, at least, art criticism) thrives on such debates, debates in which it is often difficult for outsiders to see the issues involved. For most of us the experience of art, especially of contemporary art, is something that is very difficult to verbalize, still less to fit in to an overarching understanding of social, cultural and religious trends. Indeed, the point of discussing 'The Journey' here is precisely to draw attention to the way in which – whether it 'succeeded' or not in artistic terms – it exemplifies the twin needs of artists seeking a spiritual grounding or framework for their art and of religious seekers who recognise in art (however poorly they may be able to articulate it) a fellow-traveller on the way. 'The Journey' created an opportunity for experiencing the encounter with art as a dimension of the other journey, the way of the pilgrim, on which Christians believe themselves to be engaged.

From what has been said it will be clear that 'The Journey' contained few works with an explicitly Christian content. The spiritual quest it exemplified was in large part diffuse and unfocused. It might, therefore, be useful to turn to another recent exhibition, 'Images of Christ', held in

Northampton and in the crypt of St Paul's Cathedral, which specifically (as its title indicates) looked at the representation of Christ in post-war British art. 'Images of Christ' marked the centenary of St Matthew's Church in Northampton and paid tribute to its former Vicar, Walter Hussey, who is widely regarded (and who seemed to have regarded himself) as one of the last great ecclesiastical patrons of art (*Patron of Art* was the title he gave to his autobiography). His achievement was certainly remarkable. At St Matthew's and later at Chichester Cathedral he commissioned artists of the stature of Henry Moore, Graham Sutherland, Benjamin Britten and Leonard Bernstein – often at astonishingly low prices! The exhibition managed to find 'images of Christ' made by leading artists of the post-war period – Henry Moore and Graham Sutherland (inevitably) but also Jacob Epstein, Stanley Spencer, Elisabeth Frink, Edward Burra, Antony Caro and others – as well as by a larger number of more 'minor' figures ranging from Beryl Cook (well-known for her popular and colourful pictures of seaside landladies, etc.) through artists known for their Church commissions such as Hans Feibusch and Peter Ball to contemporaries such as Albert Herbert, whose work is highly regarded within the art world but little-known outside.

If this seems like a long list of names, that is partly the point: it is very easy to bewail the decline of religious art in the twentieth century, yet not only do many younger artists (such as those featured in 'The Journey') seek a spiritual value in and through their work but others continue to find in the Christian story a powerful theme for their work.

This statement, however, should be qualified by two comments. The first is that, as Paul Tillich noted some time ago, the main 'point of contact' between art and the gospel in our time is in the symbol of the cross: the passion of Christ is particularly prominent in these pictures, and although there are, of course, other reasons why a Church commission may be more likely, statistically speaking, to require 'a cruci-fixion', it is hard to avoid the reflection that the suffering and death of Christ are used by artists as a vehicle by which to express twentieth century angst, desperation and the human suffering of two world wars and continuing abuses of human rights. In the works shown by Stanley Spencer and Anthony Green, for example, the crucifixion is almost transparently used for making a highly personal and histrionic statement about the artist himself that seems to trivialize the subject. Edward Burra's 'Christ Mocked', in which the sadistic, even the demonic, aspect of the subject is powerfully stated, could not be accused of trivialization – but there is nothing 'redemptive' about the cruelty we are confronted with. Similarly, Sutherland's great 'Crucifixion' painted for St Matthew's Church in the immediate aftermath of the war, is a sombre testimony to what, in the war, 'man has made of man'. In this perspective the suffering and dying Christ is the twentieth century's 'Everyman'. The Christian 'symbols of glory', however, are conspicuously lacking. We might compare this situation with that of the nineteenth century, when scenes from the childhood and ministry of Jesus were used by prominent artists such as Holman Hunt, Millais, and others. Such scenes, however, were almost entirely lacking from 'Images of Christ', a fact which says a lot about the twentieth century and about the way in which art and Christianity interact in our time.

The other comment is that although leading artists are still surprisingly willing to address Christian themes if they are given the opportunity, it is only rarely that that is the real centre of the work and still rarer for such works to be amongst their greater achievements. The thesis that the gulf between the Church and the studio (shall we say between Paris and Jerusalem?) is steadily widening is not conclusively proved – but it remains very plausible and a Hussey might be taken to be the exception who proves the rule.

Yet, even allowing full weight to the negative side of this debate, it is again striking that art and faith continue to make such assignations. If we say, for example, that Sutherland's 'Crucifixion' shows the twentieth century 'everyman' rather than the Christ of Christian doctrine, it is still worth pondering *why* the artist chose (or was willing) to use this particular figure by which to express the plight of the modern everyman. Moreover, the picture shows us – in the spirit of a long tradition of Christian piety – more vividly and more immediately than words can say, that in the suffering of our fellows, the concentration camp prisoners, the victims of bombings and of battlefields, we *see* Christ re-crucified, we do indeed see Christ re-crucified. Not only this: because it is unmistakably the Christ of Christian tradition who is used to represent the universal human sufferer in this way we are invited to reflect not only on 'what man has made of man' but also on 'what man has made of God'. This painting is not an argument – it is a showing and, as the Buddhist proverb has it, 'One showing is worth a thousand sayings'. Moreover, in an age in which television images of human suffering confront us night after night to the point at which it becomes almost impossible for us to absorb them any more, a painting such as this educates us in the sensibility needed to interpret such images. It is a sensibility that attends to the depth of suffering that cries out to us from them, to penetrate their humanity – and thus, also, their theology.

Outside the sphere of language, of the articulate word of preaching and teaching, of discussion and of argument, the images of art continue to supplement and augment the life of the Christian tradition. Whether it be in images of the 'structural grace in things', still-shimmering reflections of the original radiance and glory of God's good creation; whether it be in the tentative and exploratory images of those journeying in search of a faith they cannot yet name; or, whether it be in images that brand an all too recognisably human face on the Passion, visual art provides a powerful and formative dimension of Spirit-and-Tradition. As we have argued that means nothing less than the process by which the Church comes to be that which, for our time, it is.

Housing God

We turn now to what could be regarded as a special case of visual theology, yet one which has a very particular set of associations – and one liable to arouse a particular degree of passion: the theology of Church building. To some, this might seem a contradiction in terms. Don't many of the problems of the Church – and of the Church of England in particular – arise out of an almost obsessive over-identification of the Church with the building in which the Church

community meets for worship? Don't we need to stir people
to a more spiritual understanding of the word 'Church' and
rescue it from its identification with the bricks-and-mortar,
the plant? To speak about such a thing as a 'Christian' architecture might seem absurd, because, in the words of
Solomon, the great Temple-builder, 'the heavens, even the
highest heaven, cannot contain you. How much less this
Temple I have built!' (1 Kings 8.27). God, if God is in any
sense 'the Supreme Being', cannot be adequately housed or
represented by any human artefact. All we can realistically
look for from a Church building is that it provides a place in
which the worshipping community can meet, in which the
Word can be heard and the sacraments celebrated. What
'style' it affects is entirely indifferent. And yet, set against this
is the gut-feeling of many worshippers and visitors that one
building *is* conducive to worship whilst another is not, that
buildings generate a range of feeling-responses ('atmos-
pheres') some of which are more appropriate than others to
what we understand to be the requisite 'holy mood' of
worship.

The Case for Gothic

Perhaps the most obvious claimant to the title of 'Christian
architecture' (for Western Europeans, at least) is what we call
Gothic. If asked to draw a Church building, most people
would, I suspect, draw it in Gothic style. Augustus Welby
Pugin was, in the words of the *Oxford Dictionary of the
Christian Church*, 'the chief initiator and inspirer of the
"Gothic Revival".' For Pugin, religious architecture cannot
be separated from theology; and it is his view that, in particular, what we call 'Gothic' (which he himself preferred to call
'pointed architecture') has a peculiar appropriateness for use
in Church building. A typical Gothic Church, he argues, is
theological through and through, and illustrates in a very
definite way what he regards as 'the three great doctrines' of
Christianity, namely, 'the redemption of man by the sacrifice
of our Lord on the cross; the three equal persons united in
the Godhead; and the resurrection of the dead.'[7]
 How, we may ask, does it do all this?

To begin with the cross: the cross, according to Pugin, 'is not only the very plan and form of a Catholic Church, but it terminates each spire and gable, and is imprinted as a seal of faith on the very furniture of the altar'. Next, the Trinity: this, Pugin claims, 'is fully developed in the triangular form and arrangement of arches, tracery and even subdivisions of the buildings themselves'. Lastly, the resurrection of the dead 'is beautifully exemplified by great height and vertical lines, which have been considered by the Christians from the earliest period, as the emblem of the resurrection'. (This latter principle is also, in his view, exemplified by the Early Church's custom of standing for prayers during the Easter season and led to the adoption of the pointed arch itself.) We may note that with regard to these three symbolic functions only the first – that which has to do with the cross – is directly representational; the symbolisation of the Trinity and of the resurrection has more to do with elements of structural design and unconscious effect. Here is how he describes the overall effect of a Church built in the Gothic style:

> Do not all the features and details of the Churches erected during the Middle Ages, set forth their origin, and, at the same time, exhibit the triumphs of Christian truth? Like the religion itself, their foundations are on the cross and they rise from it in majesty and glory. The lofty nave and choir, with still loftier towers, crowned by clusters of pinnacles and spires, all directed towards heaven, beautiful emblems of the Christian's brightest hope, the shame of the Pagan; the cross, raised on high in glory, – a token of mercy and forgiveness, – crowning the sacred edifice, and placed between the anger of God and the sins of the city.[8]

Far from being neutral, merely a matter of custom and convenience, architectural style is so integral to the life of the worshipping community that, for Pugin, a change of style implies nothing less than a change in theology and that, consequently, to abandon the achievements of pointed architecture is to abandon the faith itself. Writing of the change from Gothic to classical models in the Renaissance he said, 'The change which took place in the sixteenth century was not a matter of mere taste, but a change of soul; it was a great contention between Christian and pagan ideas, in which the latter triumphed ... from the moment the Christians adopted this fatal mistake, of reviving classic design, the principles of architecture have been thrown into miserable confusion.'[9] And not only the principles of architecture, but the religious life of the Church itself; for Pugin saw what he regarded as the degeneration of contemporary Church life as vitally connected to the degeneration of the architectural setting of worship. A Church which could be satisfied with what he called 'the Commissioners' Style' (the neo-classical style widely used by the Church Commissioners in a programme of building new Churches for the expanding urban population) was not, as he understood the case, a Church that knew its own gospel.

There have, of course, been other notable presentations of the case for Gothic which have not pursued Pugin's narrowly theological line. John Ruskin was equally strong in his support for Gothic, but he emphasised its conformity to natural archtypes and forms. 'All most lovely forms and thoughts,' he said, 'are directly taken from natural objects' and it is our preceding response to the natural archetypes that predisposes us to value those works of art that reflect or embody them. Thus, the Gothic arch affects us so deeply not, as Pugin argued, because of its doctrinal content (as a symbol of the resurrection), but, in Ruskin's own words, 'because its form is one of those which, as we know by its frequent occurrence in the work of Nature around us, has been appointed by the Deity to be an everlasting source of pleasure to the human mind.'[10] God's universal revelation in Nature, the divine traces left by the Creator in his creation, take priority – for art and architecture – over the more specific revelation enshrined in Christian doctrine. Similarly, the proportions of Gothic architecture work for us and on us because of their resonance with the proportions of natural forms – not because they directly represent revealed truths such as the triune nature of God.

Others have defended Gothic on the basis of a historical vision that sees this architecture as the product of a 'unanimous society', a society in which, in the words of Eric Gill, 'there is one mind, one attitude towards life, one pervading sense of its meaning, a universal acceptance of a certainly defined finality, and that finality, that final cause, God, a final cause outside material life, but pervading, directing and ruling it.'[11] Such a social order was, Gill believed, a precondition for the creation of any good art, religious or other, and was a condition that the Middle Ages possessed but we have lost.

Note that here – although there is nothing from which Pugin would dissent – the point is not the detail of how the architecture represents or pictures theological truth, but the religious spirit of the age which produced these buildings, as that is reflected in the beauty of the final product. It is not a question of the architecture acting as a kind of code or language stating a sequence of very specific doctrines (as it might be in Pugin's presentation of the case) but more a matter of expressing the faith of the builders.

However the case for Gothic is made it is, as I have suggested, perhaps the front runner, as far as the West is concerned, for the title of 'Christian architecture'. John Henry Newman probably spoke for many when he suggested that Gothic possesses 'a commanding beauty, such as no other style possesses with which we are acquainted, and which probably the Church will not see surpassed till it attain to the Celestial City.'[12]

The Case for Classicism

Although the Gothic Revival had considerable success in shaping our view of what counts as 'good' Church architecture, other arguments and other experiences have also had their representatives in recent years. The 1980s, for example, saw something of a neo-classical revival, encouraged – amidst much controversy – by the Prince of Wales, whose *Vision of Britain* and associated remarks about modernist 'carbuncles' won widespread support amongst the public and widespread criticism from professional architects. Quinlan Terry, perhaps the best-known contemporary British architect linked to this classical revival, has also come in for sharp criticism from colleagues. Some have connected the apparent conservatism of his architecture and his opinions with the political conservatism of the 1980s.

Nonetheless, Terry was appointed to design the new Roman Catholic cathedral of St Helen's, Brentwood, which thereby became the first Cathedral Church in classical style to be built in Britain since St Paul's.

Terry is not himself a Roman Catholic, indeed, having been brought to Christianity by the Welsh Calvinistic Methodist preacher Dr Martyn Lloyd Jones he comes from a quite distinct theological tradition. He does not seek to create 'sacred space' and is not sympathetic to the use of images in religion. The main requirement of a Church building in his view is that it should enable the Word to be preached and heard. Yet he has a fascinating, if idiosyncratic, vision of the origins of classicism which link it very closely to the origins of Christianity and suggest a profound harmony between classical structures and Christianity.

Terry rejects the customary account of the origins of the classical orders found in Vitruvius, whom he describes as 'a good party-line Roman'[13], ideologically committed to the view 'that the Imperial style was rooted in the Imperial religion' (ibid.), thus overlooking the true origins of classicism – in the despised history of one of Rome's subject peoples: the Jews. For, according to Terry, the true origins of classicism are described in Exodus, chapters 35–9, when Moses instructs Bezaleel and Aholiab in the construction of the Tabernacle, according to the model revealed to him by God: 'the *visual form* of the building in which the one true God was to be worshipped, could not be left to the vain imagination of man, so a detailed description was given to Moses' (AR, p. 29). 'What we were given in the beginning by divine inspiration is the perfect combination of natural forms with the wisdom of sensible construction and the skill of the craftsman. This is the essence of classical orders and indeed of all architecture.'[14] But, 'who would believe,' he asks, 'that an obscure shepherd leading a band of wandering exiles through the Wilderness of Arabia should devise the perfect set of architectural principles which survived, world-wide, through all man-made fashions and conceits?' (AR, p. 33).

Terry maintains that there is a universal quality in classical style that maintains itself in the midst of all the variations to which it is historically subject – even Gothic is, according to Terry, 'really a form of classical' (RIBA, p. 9). Like nature itself it provokes 'awe and admiration', and is capable of giving expression to 'all historical periods, national characteristics, political systems and even personal moods of individual architects and yet preserve[s its] principles and remain[s] neutral' (AR, p. 29). Such architecture obeys 'the first and greatest commandment in architecture', namely, 'to strive after beauty; that beauty and repose which we find so satisfying in the natural world around us and which is so evident in the great buildings and art of the past' (RIBA, p. 12).

Architecture's fall from grace was seen by Pugin to have occurred in the classical triumph of the renaissance. Terry identifies this fall with the rise of modernism, 'an alien culture brutally thrusting itself into the history of architecture' (RIBA, p. 8). Modernism, he says, is the architectural manifestation of the Victorian 'belief in the *inevitability of change*, as introduced by Darwin and propagated by Marx', a belief which carries with it 'a contempt for the past and ... blind faith in the future. It spurns anything that smacks of nationality or individuality, the spiritual world of the historic past. It is the expression of the Darwinian *homo sapiens*; man, produced by a seeming accident of time, without sin, guilt, or soul, or relationship to his Maker, or fear of death. Such a man, stripped of all his virtues and vices must be equal to everyone else and international – a veritable Mr Average' (RIBA, p. 9).

The Case for Modernism

It is hard to see Terry and Pugin agreeing on much – except, perhaps, on this: that modernism is of all styles that least fitted for the service of the Church. Modernism seems to represent the antithesis of what we regard as Church architecture. Urban visitors to country churches have been known to say of their own post-war church building that, in comparison with its rural counterparts, theirs is not 'a real church'. Yet the modernist movement has made an important impact on church architecture, and there are arguments to suggest that this is not simply a matter of indifferently using the prevailing or current mode of architecture but of making use of a significant match between architectural style and theological content.

Widely acclaimed as one of the most 'successful' churches built in the twentieth century, the pilgrim church of Notre-Dame-du-Haut at Ronchamp in France, replacing an earlier structure destroyed by shelling in the closing stages of the war, and its architect Le Corbusier offer a useful starting-point for considering the case for modernism in church architecture.

Le Corbusier never claimed to be a Christian believer, although, in the way of many artistic modernists, he was in a general sense 'religious' and both his life and work express a certain 'spirituality'. He said of himself 'I am religious. That is to say, I can believe in some gigantic ideal which dominates me and which I can hope to achieve.'[15] Coming from an almost puritanical Swiss Protestant background much of his youthful reading of late romantic, early modernist works (including both Ruskin and Nietzsche) nurtured an aspiration to a spirituality of unity, wholeness, harmony with creation (or, the cosmos), the bringing together of the material and the spiritual worlds and a feeling for the ineffable mystery working in and through the universe of visible forms. He respected the disciplined solitude and austerity of the monks whom he visited on Mount Athos and the French Dominicans for whom he built a new monastery and there was, as several commentators have noted, something monastic, something ascetic about his own life-style. He was also to find a champion in Jean Marie-Alain Couturier, a Catholic priest, and editor of the pro-modernist journal L'Art Sacré. Something of Le Corbusier's undogmatic but profoundly held spirituality can be glimpsed in such statements as: 'A man who searches for harmony has a sense of the sacred. There are some things which you don't have the right to violate: the secret which is in every being, a great limitless void where you either can or cannot place your own notion of the sacred – individual, completely individual. This is also called conscience and it is the tool of measurement of responsibility or of feelings, reaching out to the graspable or ineffable.'[16] A philosopher or theologian might find the terminology and expression confused – but the feeling is clear and patently sincere!

Ronchamp was not the first religious project to engage Le Corbusier. Immediately after the war he had become involved in a grandiose scheme to build an underground Cathedral in the South of France, at a site associated in legend with Mary Magdalene. The kind of tension so characteristic of the relationship between the Catholic hierarchy and the modernist movement came to expression in the response of a special conclave of cardinals and archbishops. 'The cardinals and archbishops,' a press report stated, 'are unanimous in condemning this initiative and do not approve any appeal made to the generosity of Catholics in support of this project.' The scheme came to nothing.

Nonetheless, when the good offices of Couturier led to Le Corbusier being approached to undertake the building of the new Church at Ronchamp he responded with a brilliant and unique design. Sited (as its name suggests) on a hill-top, Notre-Dame-des-Hauts is distinguished by a roof which rises on the south side – the side seen by approaching pilgrims – to a wave-like crest, supported by curved walls, in which are set deep, irregularly placed and variously sized windows of non-representative coloured glass. On the inside this contributes to the atmosphere of peace, calm, silence – and, in the experience of many visitors, joy and prayer, something that even photographs suggest. 'A sense of the sacred,' he is reported as saying, 'animated our effort.'[17]

Le Corbusier understood his work to be developed in accord with natural principles and with a respectful eye to the specific landscape environment of the building. For sacredness, in his sense, is rooted in the harmony between man-made and natural form and in the power of both to evoke mystery. As a key to good form Le Corbusier (who shared with Terry a dislike of the metric system) developed a method of measuring which he called the 'modulor'. This is an attempt to embody a common denominator between human proportion and elemental geometry. Whatever the results of applying the modulor, the principle itself is reminiscent of Ruskin's quest for a system of architectural proportions based on proportions found in nature: indeed, we might pause to reflect that apologists of Gothic, classicism and modernism alike appeal to nature for validation of their methods! Not that Le Corbusier was blind to the beauties of Gothic: in a work entitled *Quand les Cathedrales étaient Blanches* (*When the Cathedrals were White*) he praises the medieval cathedrals as an example of a truly international style, expressing the spirit of a free and unanimous population in contrast to the chaotic sprawl of, say, Manhattan. He also reminds readers that when they were first built these cathedrals would have looked very different from the weather-beaten piles with which we are familiar. Their newness and whiteness would have made them stand out with all the purity and cleanness of form that he sought in contemporary building.

It is perhaps worth noticing, in comparing and contrasting the claims of modernism and classicism that they seem, in Church building, to be aiming at two very different goals. For classicism – at least as interpreted by Terry – the aim is not to make a 'sacred' space nor to evoke mystery and awe. Rather, the intention is to build a rational and well-ordered space in which the Word can be ministered. Le Corbusier's church building ideals, on the other hand, reveal what we might call the mythological dimension of modernism: its quest for a non-doctrinal level of mystery and primitive sacrality – the same motivation that led Picasso and other early modernists in painting to rediscover so-called 'primitive' art. It is an interesting point to consider to what extent such a dimension of mystery (what the theologian Rudolf Otto called 'the numinous') is or isn't integral to Christianity and whether it is or isn't a valid aim of church architecture.

This last point might be qualified by adding that for modernism the sense of the sacred is paradoxically connected with the experience of the absence of God. The emptiness, plain materials, bare surfaces and stark outlines of modernist architecture are conceived as 'a holy silence before the Word'. Writing of the Church of Corpus Christi in Aachen, dating from 1930 and one of Germany's first 'modernist' churches, Tim Gough has said 'The architect intended the tall, totally bare white wall beyond the altar to be the strongest figurative representation. The "beyond" of the altar is acknowledge in a reticence that is itself an indication of modern man's hesitation in representating the transcendent explicitly.'[18] We can imagine that someone used to the many theological pointers to be found in a traditional church might have a sense that 'there's something missing' in such a bare interior: but that, it seems, is the point. As an architecture reflecting a period in which the Church has produced both the absolute insistence on divine transcendence and otherness to be found in Karl Barth's early writings *and* theologies of the death or absence of God. In this architecture it's precisely transcendence-to-the-point-of-absence that's being aimed at.

The Church in History

We have now looked at 'apologies' for three very different kinds of church architecture. Naturally, this does not represent an exhaustive commentary on all possible styles. Some will regret that nothing has been said about one of the most profound and moving of all styles – Romanesque, a style that Bishop John Tinsley, in an outstanding essay, has described as possessing 'a genuine theology of the secular'.[19] But it has not been our intention to be exhaustive. Our aim has been more modest: to show how questions of architectural style can, for good or ill, be 'theologised'. Naturally, it is relatively rare for a church building to represent any one style in a pure form although, of course, it is the case that some churches – whether by Pugin, Terry or Le Corbusier – are built to a very definite 'plan' and are intended to embody a very definite architectural 'programme'. At the same time, a church is also a communal building and, as such, shares in the continuing life of the community it serves. It follows that any church building which survives for more than one or two generations will start to bear the marks of history, whether these are constructive (that is, decorations or extensions added to the initial structure) or destructive (as in the case of those churches subject to the iconoclasm of the Puritans in the English Civil War). Allan Doig, in an editorial in the journal *Church Building* speaks of the church building as a 'palimpsest' of the life of the community, that is to say, a manuscript that has been written over many times in such a way that beneath the most recent level of writing one can still make out at least fragments of earlier messages. 'The building,' he says, 'is an existential trace of the worshipping community. The church has grown with them, has been shaped by them, been overlaid with their memorials and with their symbols.' [20] Perhaps, then, when an urban Christian, served by a post-war church building says that it's 'not a real church' compared with, for example, an ancient village church, they're not making a specifically architectural point; that is to say, they're not stating a preference for Gothic over against modernism. What they might be expressing is the sense of history, the feeling for the continuity of the community 'through many dangers, toils and snares' that is recorded in the Church building. For such a church – no matter how 'ordinary' from the point of view of an architectural historian – cannot but evoke rich associations. The groove in the stone steps down which one enters has been worn by centuries of worshippers and visitors, from the Middle Ages to the present, contemporaries of the Black Prince, of Shakespeare, Jane Austen, Dickens and Churchill; knights and ladies, serfs and villeins, Tudor yeomen and Puritan soldiers, dissolute squires and reformed sinners, Tractarian clergymen and Elvis fans, soldiers and sailors returning from wars against Spain, against the United States, against Napoleon, the Czar, the Kaiser, the Führer or General Galtieri; dressed variously in wimples, ruffs, wigs, bonnets, bustles, frock coats and flares, they have all been here before us, adoring the sacrament or seeking justification by faith, singing and reciting hymns, psalms and prayers, listening to intoned Latin masses, hour-long sermons and Stanford in G; some were devout, some were bored, some indifferent or uncomprehending – but their stories are all part of the building and even though you don't know them you *feel* them as you enter by the way they entered and kneel where they knelt.

But the Church building is not merely evidence for the secular history that is the background of the Christian story. It is also itself a prime example of how change works within the Church, a never-ending story of adaptations and alterations, reflecting both the wider life of society – its wars, its economic booms, its revolutions – and the Church's own internal development, embodying traces of Reformation, of Puritanism, of the Evangelical Revival and of the Oxford Movement as well as of more recent currents in theology and spirituality. May not the very natural, spontaneous pleasure which people of quite varied cultural backgrounds find in such buildings act as a warning to those who want to create places for communal worship in the light of any single overriding architectural or theological doctrine. It has been said that 'the basic character of a farmhouse says a great deal more about the "spirit" of the land, and a style of building reveals more of the basic philosophy of a period than the carefully smoothed-out texts of that time ...'[21] In agreeing with this remark we would also like to suggest that the basic character of an ancient church as 'a palimpest' of the ever-changing life community helps us to experience something of the reality of tradition, of the continuous, seamless network of interactions between individuals and between generations, between local practices and the wider Church, between Church and society (indeed, the Church building is the most obvious 'mediator' between Church and society). In such a building spontaneous expressions of piety mix with inspiration from theological theory. This is arguably the most material sign of what it means for the Church in its tradition, in the process of receiving-and-delivering the faith, to become local, specific, subject for our sake to time, space and history.

Ever Singing

If the visual arts have frequently faced theological opposition from within the Church, music seems to have fared much better. The gospels record Jesus and his disciples singing together after the Last Supper, while the Letter to the Colossians commands its readers to 'sing psalms, hymns and spiritual songs with gratitude in your hearts to God' (Col. 3.16). Since then the Church, even the Church of the Puritans, has been 'ever singing', permitting, encouraging and even demanding the cultivation of music as an integral part of worship. We have a Royal School of Church Music – but no Royal School of Church Art! Whereas it is possible to argue that much of the religious art produced in the twentieth century has been either the best work of second-rate artists or the second-rate work of first-rate artists (not an argument we accept – but one that could be put), musical settings of liturgical and other religious texts continue to attract the best contemporary musicians. In the twentieth century Britain alone can furnish such examples as Elgar, Holst, Vaughan Williams and (again, on one occasion, in collaboration with Walter Hussey) Benjamin Britten. Amongst contemporary composers John Tavener, Jonathan Harvey and Arvo Pärt (an Estonian who has produced work for British Churches) might be mentioned. Hand in hand with this, the Church's own musical tradition generates works that, if not always accepted by critics as fully mainstream, demand respectful attention.

It is in this respect instructive to consider the case of Herbert Howells, the centenary of whose birth was celebrated in 1992. At the time of that centenary Howells was described in the *Independent on Sunday* (11.10.92) as 'the house composer' of the 'Cathedrals of the English-speaking world', and, indeed, as a master of 'the Oxbridge Anglican aesthetic: a supreme manipulator of the theatre of transcendent ceremonial and dignified nostalgia that the Church of England does like no one else.' There is, then, a good case for taking Howells as a representative of the Church's musical tradition in twentieth century.

It is tempting to assume that this tradition, like all traditions worthy of the name 'tradition', goes back in an unbroken line of succession to some venerable past – from where we are now to such early 'greats' as Byrd, Tallis and, beyond them, to the chants of medieval monasticism, with each generation nurturing and cherishing the achievements of those who had gone before and, in doing so, grafting on their own special contribution. But, it is clear that things have not always gone that smoothly! In 1836, for instance, Augustus Welby Pugin, the Gothic revival architect, decried the degraded state of England's great ecclesiastical buildings and of the worship conducted in them. Speaking of the typical lay-clerk of a Cathedral choir, he declared that 'to such a degraded state are [they] fallen, that even the keeper of a public tavern is found among their number. Thus, this man, fresh from the fumes of the punch-bowl and tobacco-pipe, and with the boisterous calls of the tap ringing in his ears, may be seen running from the bar to the choir, there figuring away in a surplice, till the concluding prayer allows him to rush back, and mingle the response of "Coming, sir," to the amen that has hardly died away upon his lips.'[22] A not dissimilar judgement is passed by Trollope's Mr Harding, a benign clergyman who usually sees the best in everyone, but who finds little to approve in the mattins conducted in Westminster Abbey: 'Mr Harding was not much edified by the manner of the service. The minor canon in question hurried in, somewhat late in a surplice not in the neatest order and was followed by a dozen choristers who were also not as trim as they might have been. They all jostled in to their places with a quick hurried step and the service was soon commenced. Soon commenced and soon over, for there was no music and time was not unnecessarily lost in the chanting.'[23]

With such descriptions in mind we can all the more appreciate the achievements of those later Victorians who, in some respects, 'created' (or, better, re-created) the tradition which we have received; who made it possible for composers such as Howells to be so steeped in the vocabulary and the idioms of a vital, living tradition that they could use it as a starting-point, as a context, from which to explore, to express and to make through music a place in worship for passions, questions and confessions that go far beyond popular images of the complacent conformity and timorous traditionalism of the Church of England at prayer (images, perhaps, that can be sensed in the *Independent on Sunday*'s somewhat back-handed compliments).

For Howells' Church music contains the expected pomp and circumstance of Cathedral liturgy – but it contains much else besides, at times sensuous, even sweet, and often dark to the point at which doubt turns to despair. Even a musical amateur need hear only a few bars to know that, on the one hand, this is a very English music, with the safe virtues of English convention and English landscape. Yet the same few bars will also tell us that, on the other hand, this is a very twentieth century music, the music of a century which recognizes itself more readily in the symbolism of the cross than in the symbolism of religious triumphalism. The patience of the craftsman is at every moment touched by the shadow of times which saw catastrophic world wars, social revolution and private tragedy – and there are those who have spoken of Howells as the (musical) poet of death. For all men of his generation it was probably true that by the time they were thirty half their friends were dead, cut down like Howells' own close friend Ivor Gurney in the killing-fields of Europe. Moreover, most parents of his generation could expect to see at least one of their children die from such diseases as tuberculosis, polio or diphtheria, as Howells saw his nine-year old son Michael die in his arms. Such deaths, such mourning are there in the music, music like the anthem 'Take him, earth, for cherishing' commemorating the assassination of President Kennedy or the '*Hymnus Paradisi*' written in the wake of his own son's death. This is the work many judge to be his masterpiece and it is a work which confronts us with the pain of ultimate separation and ultimate loss. The same tension, however, can be sensed throughout his production – take for example, the creed from the 'Collegium Regale' Eucharistic setting.

Interestingly, as far as formal belief goes, Howells appears to have hesitated on the brink of faith, unable to affirm the hope that we shall meet again, that there will be an ultimate consolation to match the ultimate loss. In this respect he is not unlike a number of other composers of great religious music. The riddle of Mozart's personal faith has continued to perplex pious admirers, whilst, more recently one might again think of Ralph Vaughan Williams or Gabriel Fauré, whose 'Requiem' must rank as one of the most popular modern 'religious' works. Yet it is clear that Howells' music has brought strength and consolation to others – no matter what words and reasons they may have used to rationalise that strengthening. It would also seem that the process of writing it brought strength, consolation and healing in some measure to Howells himself – with whatever words and reasons *he* may have rationalized that process and that healing.

It is a common belief that the artist – painter, poet or musician –is gifted with unique opportunities to give form to our most heartfelt anxieties and pains, the ones we hide as we go about our everyday business; and yet, by giving form to the darkness, by finding the right word, the right colour, the right melody, the right chord, the artist may be able to show us the first step on the long, long journey of healing. The word, the colour, the note shaped by art can provide a first sign of hope, a rumour of spring to come. Now, it may be that the artist, as artist, can take us no further than to the edge of a hesistant agnosticism, showing us in a moment of rapture what joy, what hope, what consolation might be like, if such things are to be found in the world, but whether the joy, the hope and the consolation exist outside the moment of rapture is another matter – and here we sense the limit to the healing and the hope offered by art.

Like the minister, the artist is always in the situation of 'the wounded healer', a statement pre-eminently true of a man like Howells. Though when an artist is able to accept the teaching and the discipline of a tradition which has renewed itself from generation to generation in the flame of that rapture, then it may well be that his best achievements will not only have a quality of conviction which is more than the subjective product of an individual creative genius, but also touch on truths which may still remain in part hidden to the artist himself. The work persuades, even when the artist himself is only half-persuaded. Here, it may be is a clue, not only to the value to faith of a composer such as Howells or of the tradition he represents, but a clue to the wider issue of tradition. For although, as we have described it, the process of Spirit-and-Tradition is one in which the message must constantly be put at risk if it is to be fruitful and vital and although there is no danger-fee zone for faith, it is also true that 'not everything depends on us', that is, not on our conscious, verbalised thinking, speaking and willing. The mutual obligation of bearing one another's burdens is an obligation from which we may be – and perhaps usually are

– beneficiaries more than we are contributors. In effecting the coinherence of heaven and earth the process of Spirit-and-Tradition also effects our interdependence one on another – one more lesson in which the tacit dimension of art may better be able to instruct us than the often too public, too over-stated discourse of theology.

Chapter 8

Spirit in the World

Inside and Outside

Since its earliest days the Church has wrestled (as Israel wrestled before) with the question: What of those outside the Law? What of those whose lives are spent outside the visible community of faith? What of those who lived before the advent of Christ or who never get to hear the preaching of the Word or whose only encounter with the Church is such that the human 'husk' completely obscures the divine 'kernel' (one might, perhaps, think of a child subject to persistent sexual abuse by a priest, identified by that child as the pre-eminent local representative of the Church). Are we to say that such people (numerically speaking a massive majority of the human race) are outside the scope of redemption? Or that, even if we were to concede the possibility of a last-minute decision in their favour – solely motivated by grace – at the Last Judgement, must we then say that in the meanwhile even their virtues, their best achievements of knowledge and of action, are no more than splendid vices?

Such questions have, as already suggested, engaged the Church from the earliest times and at every stage the positions which Henry Bettenson has called 'a liberal view' and 'a negative view' have both found powerful advocates. In the New Testament itself we find texts that could be interpreted either way. We might, for example, read Jesus's words in John 10.16 as implying a 'liberal' view: 'I have other sheep that are not of this sheep pen. I must bring them also.' On the other hand, the rather more frequently quoted words from the same gospel 'I am the way and the truth, and the life. No one comes to the Father except through me' (John 14.6), have usually been taken in an opposite sense. Similarly, the powerful early chapters of Paul's Letter to the Romans offer evidence to both parties. On the one hand we find such texts as 'For since the creation of the world God's invisible qualities – his eternal power and divine nature – have been clearly seen' (Rom. 1.20), and '... when Gentiles, who do not have the law, do by nature things required by the law, they are a law for themselves ...' (Rom. 2.14–15). On the other hand Paul's description of how those who had the opportunity to know God through the ordering of creation have become 'futile' in their 'thinking', exchanging 'the glory of the immortal God for images made to look like mortal man ...' and being subsequently given over by God 'to uncleanness' would seem to suggest that, outside an explicit acceptance of the preached word of the gospel, there is little to hope for. His use, in chapter 3, of Psalm 14 – 'There is no-one righteous, not even one' – would also appear to point in a similar direction.

Moving on into the Early Church we might, with Bettenson, contrast 'the liberal view' of Justin Martyr with 'the negative view' of Tertullian. Justin, with a number of other early apologists, developed the idea that precisely because Christ is identified in the New Testament with the Word 'by whom all things are made' the possibility of some kind of knowledge of him as to be universal. 'We are taught that Christ is the first-born of God, and we have shown above that He is the reason [Word] of whom the whole human race partake, and those who live according to reason are Christian, even though they are accounted atheists. Such were Socrates and Heraclitus among the Greeks, and those like them ...'[1] Tertullian's 'negative view' can be heard in the famous rhetorical question 'What has Athens to do with Jerusalem?'

And so, we might say, the story continued. As in all such conflicts, however, the mainsteam of Christian thought has settled for what may equally well be regarded as a sensible compromise or as a sell-out, balancing the need to affirm the appearance of wisdom and goodness outside the narrow confines of the Church with the desire to preserve the distinctiveness, indeed the uniqueness, of Christian faith. This compromise is vividly captured in two images used by St Augustine, whose own journey from Manicheeism, astrology and philosophy to Christian faith shows how such issues can become existentially urgent in the processes of conversion and spiritual development. The first is when Augustine recalls the story of how the departing Israelites took with them from Egypt silver and gold, despoiling the Egyptians of their treasures (Exodus 13.35–6). He then applies this to his own reading of pagan philosophy: 'It was from the Gentiles that I had come to you, and I set my mind upon the gold which you willed your people to carry away from Egypt for, wherever it was, it was yours.'[2] 'Wherever it was, it was yours ...' Even if, as he states quite clearly throughout the passage from which these lines are taken, the pagan philosophy that had so attracted him at one stage of his development is ultimately inadequate it is still, in some sense and in some measure, impressed with the seal of God's divine ordering of the human mind. Nor, if God is truly creator and lord of the universe could it be otherwise. Yet our current capacities are also affected by the event of the fall and therefore do not truly or adequately reflect the divine image in which they were made. There is thus darkness as well as light in the pagan world, as Augustine indicates by another carefully-wrought image (alluding again to the Exodus cycle):

> It is one thing to descry the land of peace from a wooded hilltop and, unable to find the way to it, struggle on through trackless wastes where traitors and runaways, captained by their prince, who is *lion and serpent* in one, lie in wait to attack. It is another thing to follow the high road to that land of peace, the way that is defended by the care of the heavenly Commander.[3]

Here it is perhaps the negative view that is emphasised: yet even if those who seek the land of peace without the help of divine revelation are struggling 'through trackless wastes' it is still acknowledged that they are, however inadequately, struggling to find truth. Traces of God may be found everywhere and inform each and every human activity – no matter how odd or inappropriate when measured against the yardstick of Christian revelation.

If the Reformation, under the leadership of Luther and Calvin, largely espoused the negative view, teaching that the divine image in humanity had been not merely obscured but obliterated by the fall, the Anglican Reformers took a more 'liberal' approach. This approach is exemplified by the great Richard Hooker, who argued forcefully for admitting the role of reason in finding out divine laws.

> The general and perpetual voice of men is as the sentence of God himself. For that which all men have at all times learned, Nature herself must needs have taught; and God being the author of Nature, her voice is but his instrument. By her from Him we receive whatsoever in such sort we learn. Infinite duties there are, the goodness whereof is by this rule sufficiently manifested, although we had no other warrant besides to approve them.

And, commenting on Paul's recognition of conscience among the Gentiles, Hooker states:

> His meaning is, that by force of the light of Reason, wherewith God illumineth every one which cometh into the world, men being enabled to know truth from falsehood, and good from evil, do thereby learn in many things what the will of God is; which will himself not revealing by any extraordinary means unto them, but they by natural discourse attaining the knowledge thereof, seem the makers of those Laws which indeed are His, and they but only the finders of them out.[4]

From 'Reason and Revelation' to 'Spirit and Tradition'

As well as putting down a marker which all subsequent Anglican discussion has (if only unconsciously) had to take into account, Hooker's words also sum up how the issue has come to be seen in the mainstream of western theology, namely, as an issue of 'Reason and Revelation'. In other words, the question guiding the discussion has been 'How can God be known?' The 'negative view' has claimed that (to quote Emil Brunner) 'Through God alone can God be known'; that is, only a free act of self-revelation on the part of God can provide the basis for human beings' knowledge of Him. Apart from such acts of revelation – for Christians uniquely testified to by the Scriptures – our minds remain completely in the dark regarding divine things. The 'liberal view' has not necessarily denied either the possibility of the necessity of revelation for a full 'saving knowledge' of God. What it has argued is that in addition to what can only be known by revelation there are also wide regions of truth that the human mind is competent to explore and that, in the course of such exploration, some truth about God will also be found.

The history of theology has, inevitably, thrown up many variants on and many combinations of these positions and, as in so many theological debates, although the issues have now been debated for many generations the battle continues to rage with each side for ever finding fresh voices to represent it. Yet, whilst it is important to take seriously a way of putting the question that has engaged many of the best minds of the Church in many times and places, it is worth remembering that such theoretical questions never exist in a vacuum. The 'reason *vs* revelation' debate would scarcely have been the focus of such continuous passion if it had not also interacted with more immediately practical aspects of the Church's life.

It is, for example, easy to see how positions taken in this debate will influence and be influenced by such issues as the ordination of women, precisely because such issues force us to consider the fundamental resources of decision-making in the Church. Thus, if it is decided that *only* revelation is an adequate source for knowledge of God, then any argument in favour of significant change will have to justify itself in terms of the media of revelation (primarily, in this case, the Scriptures). Conversely, if it is accepted that reason is, in some contexts, an appropriate instrument by which to discover divine law, then the possibility of using 'secular' insights from the fields of psychology or sociology will not necessarily be seen as out of order.

Similarly, the way in which those 'inside' the Church view the efforts of their 'outsider' neighbours to conduct their lives within a framework constructed out of the materials of humanistic thought (or from the resources of alternative religious traditions) will also reflect something of the 'reason *vs* revelation' debate. In fact, with regard to both these points, the positions taken in that debate say a lot about the basic way in which we think of the Church and of the Church's relation to 'the world'. Are we 'inside' the Church identical with 'God's elect', 'the sheep' – whilst those 'outside' are identifiable with 'the goats'? Few go that far – though few are satisfied with a view that would allow no difference at all between 'inside' and 'outside'. (And, it has to be said, one Anglican priest at least is currently barred from preaching by his Bishop, precisely because he suggested in one sermon that the parable of the sheep and the goats indicates that there will be those 'acquitted' at the Last Judgement who have not had consciously and deliberately professed faith in Christ.) In the course of history various ways of dealing with this problem have been attempted. Classically, the distinction between the 'visible' and 'invisible' Church has been brought into play while more recently the German-American theologian Paul Tillich has spoken of the 'latent' and the 'manifest' Church and the Catholic theologian Karl Rahner contributed the notion of 'anonymous Christians'.

It would be simplistic, even dishonest, to claim to be able to 'solve' the complex of questions that these themes bring into focus. What we can say, however, is that the pattern of Spirit-and-Tradition, as a pattern of dynamic, self-transforming life, that has informed much of this essay, may usefully supplement the 'reason *vs* revelation' approach. For, as we have already noticed, the 'reason *vs* revelation' approach is determined by a primary interest in *knowledge*, in what can be known of God and how it can be known. The liberal 'reason' view typically founders on the challenge as to how knowledge that is not based on revelation, that is not a direct gift of God, can, in any real sense, be called 'saving' knowledge. Having a true knowledge of the laws by which God has chosen to regulate the world-order is one thing; having the kind of knowledge that brings us into a loving, worshipping relation to God in his own person is another. It was precisely this point which Karl Barth (perhaps the most powerful exponent of the 'negative view' in the twentieth century) pressed against Emil Brunner's distinction between 'general' and 'special' revelation. 'There is,' he stated, 'no point of contact for the redeeming action of God. The new creation is in no sense the perfection of the old but rather the replacement of the old man by the new.'[5] The only possible 'point of contact', he went on to say, would be one that is created by the person of the Holy Spirit – reason and knowledge will never be enough. For Barth it would, moreover, seem that the Holy Spirit is exclusively tied to the written word of scripture and the preaching of the Church.

But this is where our model might hope to offer a way forward. Perhaps for the moment, however, we would do best to make our point in the form of a question: is it possible to think of manifestations of the Spirit 'outside' the Church, outside the sphere in which tradition maintains the vitalizing memory of Christ incarnate and resurrected? To be able to answer that question in the affirmative, to be able to say, 'Yes, there is a presence, a work, an activity of the Spirit outside the Church', would clearly take us much further than merely saying, 'Reason is sufficient to find out for itself a certain number of the divine laws which God has implanted in his creation'. This second affirmation, the affirmation concerning reason, may be 'liberal' – but it does not say how such knowledge is creative of personal faith. To be involved in the action of the Spirit, however, is already to be caught up into that great movement of life that is the love-relationship between creature and creator, creator and creature. It is already to be standing within the realm of the holy, of salvation – even if the person who thus stands does not *know* what is going on. In other words, to move from talk of 'reason' to talk of 'Spirit' is also to begin to talk in the language of personality, of love; and, whereas knowledge without love is, from the Christian point of view, a highly dubious acquisition, love without knowledge is, if less than perfect, nonetheless both real and effective.

Spirit in the World

There are precedents for the way we are now going. Spirit-talk was, for instance, almost universal in the nineteenth century. Coming out of the great flowering of philosphical and artistic idealism at the turn of the eighteenth and nineteenth centuries the evolution of the universe, the history of humanity and the growth and development of individuals and societies were all spoken of as manifestations of Spirit.

We might, for example, think of Shelley in his 'Queen Mab':

> Spirit of Nature! thou
> Life of interminable multitudes;
>   Soul of those mighty spheres
> Whose changeless paths through Heaven's deep silence lie;
>   Soul of that smallest being,
>   The dwelling of whose life
> Is one faint April sun-gleam; –
>   Man, like these passive things,
> Thy will unconsciously fulfilleth:
>   Like theirs, his age of endless peace,
>   Which time is fast maturing,
>   Will swiftly, surely come;
> And the unbounded frame, which thou pervadest,
>   Will be without a flaw
> Marring its prefect symmetry.

Or the lines from Ralph Waldo Emerson's essay on Nature –

> Spirit that lurks each form within
> Beckons to spirit of its kin;
> Self-kindled every atom glows,
> And hints the future which it owes.

– thoughts which Emerson spells out at greater length in his *Miscellanies*:

[Nature] always speaks of Spirit. It suggests the absolute ... The aspect of nature is devout. Like the figure of Jesus, she stands with bended head, and hands folded upon the breast. The happiest man is he who learns from nature the lesson of worship.

Of that ineffable essence which we call Spirit, he that thinks most will say least. We can foresee God in the coarse, as it were, distant phenomena of matter; but both language and thought desert us, and we are as helpless as fools and savages. That essence refuses to be recorded in propositions ... [but] It is the organ through which the universal spirit speaks to the individual, and strives to lead back the individual to it.[6]

Like many of their nineteenth century fellows who spoke so lyrically and enthusiastically of 'Spirit', neither Shelley nor Emerson were particularly concerned with the boundaries set by Christian orthodoxy. Indeed the special associations of 'Spirit' language with nature, on the one hand, and poetry and art, on the other, would tend to lay passages such as we have quoted open to charges of pantheism, of identifying 'spirit' with the processes of nature – rather than as a fully personal member of the divine Trinity!

Does this mean that we must completely rebuff the romantic attempt to trace the operations of Spirit all the way down to the very deepest, the most basic structures and elements of life? What of the insights of those theologians who have endeavoured to claim such language for the Church and to integrate it within the overall scheme of Christian theology? We might, for example, think of the Jesuit palaeontologist and theologian, Teilhard de Chardin, who discerned two kinds of energy as being interdependently involved at every level of cosmic and evolutionary life. He called these the material and the spiritual energy (or the 'without' and the 'within' of things) that, though in some respects opposite, must be taken together and treated as complementary if we are ever to have a full and adequate explanation of the phenomenon of life.

Although Teilhard's vocabulary was singularly obscure he did on occasion express his essential thoughts in a relatively simple manner. For example, he makes use of the saying 'To think we must eat' to explore the relationship between the two energies. 'That blunt statement,' he comments, 'expresses a whole economy, and reveals, according to the way we look at it, either the tyranny of matter or its spiritual power.' He goes on to say that,

> The loftiest speculation, the most burning love are, as we know only too well, accompanied and paid for by an expenditure of physical energy. Sometimes we need bread, sometimes wine, sometimes a drug or a hormone injection, sometimes the stimulation of a colour, sometimes the magic of a sound which goes in at our ears as a vibration and reaches our brains in the form of inspiration.

On the other hand

> ... what a variety of thoughts we get out of one slice of bread! Like the letters of the alphabet, which can equally well be assembled into nonsense as into the most beautiful poem, the same calories seem as indifferent as they are necessary to the spiritual values they nourish.

His conclusion therefore is that 'The two energies ... spread respectively through the two layers of the world (the *within* and the *without*) ... are constantly associated and in some ways pass into each other [although] it seems impossible to establish a simple correspondence between their curves.'[7]

In the visionary language of his meditation on 'The Spiritual Power of Matter' he calls on us never to despise matter, but, on the contrary, to

> ... bathe ... in the ocean of matter; plunge into it where it is deepest and most violent; struggle in its currents and drink of its waters. For it cradled you long ago in your preconscious existence; and it is that ocean that will raise you up to God.

In the 'Hymn to Matter' that follows, a Hymn in which Teilhard invokes a blessing on matter:

> You I acclaim as the inexhaustible potentiality for existence and transformation wherein the predestined substance germinates and grows.
>
> I acclaim you as the universal power which brings together and unites, through which the multitudinous monads are bound together and in which they all converge on the way of the spirit.
>
> I acclaim you as the melodious fountain of water whence spring the souls of men and as the limpid crystal whereof is fashioned the new Jerusalem.
>
> I acclaim you as the divine *milieu*, charged with creative power, as the ocean stirred by the Spirit, as the clay moulded and infused with life by the incarnate Word.[8]

Both these passages refer back to the creation narrative of Genesis 1, Teilhard's 'ocean' here standing for 'the deep', across the face of which, we are told, the Spirit moved in the very beginning of creation. In the closing words quoted from the 'Hymn to Matter' he links – in fully orthodox fashion – both Spirit and Word in this primordial creative work.

Similar calls to recognise the presence of Spirit in the work of creation – and, by implication, to acknowledge a continuing presence of Spirit in the deep structures of the natural world – have been made by many other theological writers. John V. Taylor, in his influential study *The Go-Between God*, develops a doctrine of Spirit by using the analogy of a living, growing organism, looking at different aspects of the Spirit's person as so many stages of life: annunciation, conception, gestation, labour, birth, breath, etc. It is under the rubric 'conception' that he deals with the creative aspect of the

Spirit, pulling together both biblical evidence and testimonies from those working in contemporary science to propose a vision of the Spirit as one who is present:

> ... deep within the fabric of the universe ... as the Go-Between who confronts each isolated spontaneous particle with the beckoning reality of the larger whole and so compels it to relate to others in a particular way; ... it is he who at every stage lures the inert organisms forward by giving an inner awareness and recognition of the unattained.[9]

Such theological visions do not, of course, solve any of the questions of science. The presence of the Holy Spirit in creation cannot be used as a hypothesis that might help us to by-pass the slow, patient work of collating and analysing data under conditions of the strictest exactitude. What they do do is, firstly, to recall us to that fundamental sense of spiritual awe in the face of the universe when every scientific explanation has been worked through and exhausted – or, more precisely, the awe that accompanies every intricate detail of the scientific revelation of the universe's infinite complexity; and, secondly, they remind us that our own religious longings, questings, practices and utterances can never be torn out of what Teilhard calls both the natural and the divine *milieu*. The religious person is not other than the biological person. All the physical, biological processes of being and of development remain the sustaining ground-bass of everything we do in the 'spiritual' sphere. Moreover, it is not as in some kinds of natural theology where reason is 'allowed' its own sphere of operations alongside but ultimately indifferent to the spiritual realm. It is rather that, in a manner prior to what can be found out and known consciously by reason, we are always already in a situation that is spiritually charged. In other words, by emphasising the role of the Spirit in creation (remembering that this is the same Spirit we have understood as being active in the communication of, for example, tradition and sacrament) we are implying an understanding of human life in which reason, the intellect, is no longer privileged as the main 'point of contact' (in Barth's sense) between human beings and God. The God-relationship is involved in the most primitive aspects of our being as creatures and as human creatures.

There will be those who regard this as opening the door to some kind of determinism, a subjection of the freedom of human beings to physical or biological processes, a belittling of the mind in favour of the body, going against the grain of millenia of religious thought. But the point is not to replace an over-valued intellect with an over-valued body. The point is to articulate a position that at every level does justice to the unity of the human person and of the constant interaction between divinity, nature and humanity in the development of that person.

Spirit and Human Spirit

Moving from the realms of fundamental science to those of human psychology, we turn again to Jung for a very important statement of this unitary vision. Jung broke with his 'master' Sigmund Freud precisely over the issue of spirituality. Jung, who had been seen by Freud himself as 'heir apparent' to the leadership of the psycho-analytic school, became increasingly unhappy with Freud's endeavour to reduce everything to sexuality. 'Above all,' he wrote,

> Freud's attitude towards the spirit seemed to me highly questionable. Wherever, in a person or in a work of art, an expression of spirituality (in the intellectual, not the supernatural sense) came to light, he suspected it, and insinuated that it was represeed sexuality ... I protested that this hypothesis, carried to its logical conclusion, would lead to an annihilating judgement upon culture. Culture would then appear as a mere farce, the morbid consequence of repressed sexuality. 'Yes,' he assented, 'so it is ...' [10]

Of course Jung here demurs from claiming to talk about 'Spirit' in a supernatural sense, but it is nonetheless clear from many of his works (and, perhaps even more importantly, from his own practice as a healer) that he was committed to making room for all those religious phenomena that Freud wanted to jettison as remnants of outmoded superstition and sexual repression. No less than Freud, Jung understood the human person as a continuum, developing out of and ultimately inseparable from the bodily roots of its being. But this did not, in his view, debar the validity of religious experience and, in a very broad sense, 'spirituality'. He speaks of the 'unbearable contradiction' that arises if we go on thinking in terms of the 'mind *vs* matter' debate. Instead he presses for a recognition of 'the mysterious truth that spirit is the living body seen from within, and the body the outer manifestation of the living spirit'.[11]

If, in this way, all human life is already in some degree or in a certain aspect 'spiritual', there may nonetheless be certain activities or forms of behaviour in which this spiritual presence is more explicitly focussed. It is telling that one volume in Jung's collected works is entitled *The Spirit in Man: Art and Literature*. For artistic creativity would appear to involve just that kind of concentrated, spontaneous yet well-ordered release of energy that we find involved in what the religious tradition says of Spirit manifestations. Art begins far below the threshold (or, we might say, well beyond the frontier) that marks the limit of reason. An artist doesn't *know*, cannot *explain*, why this image or that word is the image that must be made or the word that must be spoken in this place, at this time and in this way. Art is active and expressive as the life, the movements, the gestures of the body are active and expressive (and usually involves, to a very high degree, the physical co-operation of the body). Art has both suddenness and power that defy intellectual rationalization or explanation. And yet, art is also profoundly *human*, profoundly *meaningful*, eloquent of who we really are.

Even so, to limit the activity of Spirit in the world to such creativity, or to allow the artist any kind of qualitative superiority over ordinary mortals as a specially privileged bearer of Spirit – no matter how splendid or astonishing the works in which that artistry is manifest – would be to fall far short of the vision we are now seeking. To establish the existence of a special 'spiritual élite' outside the Church (the community of artists and art-lovers, let us say) is no less – and in many respects far more – scandalous than to limit the operation of the Spirit to the sphere of the visible or manifest Church. The vision of Spirit 'outside' the Church which we are seeking is far more fundamental than that. It is a vision for which 'all human life is here' – here, that is, in the never-ending story of God's ever-new dealings in and with 'all that is, seen and unseen'. The furthest reaches of matter and the most untalented of individuals, the good, the bad and the ugly as well as the beautiful people, are all in this story, in this sharing and communication of life.

If all this (if any of this) is true, then we need a new sensitivity to what Paul Tillich called 'the spiritual presence' outside the Church. For if there is such a presence and if it is as intimately and as universally involved in human life as has been suggested, then there can be no prior limits on the forms that such presence can take, there can be no restriction of the possibilities of new and unexpected revelations to the relatively safe and comfortable guidelines laid down by natural law. This is not to denigrate in any way the patient and painstaking quest by science to discover the universal laws of nature operative in each and every dimension of life – from the awesome mysteries of the 'Big Bang' through the complexities of genetic codes to the universes disclosed in the sub-atomic world. Nor is it to disregard the search for comparable natural laws in the human sciences, where we may think, for example, of those jurists who seek, by means of universal principles of justice, to provide a framework for the safeguarding of human rights. Rationality has its justification, and we would not wish to undermine the need for the careful weighing and analysis of evidence in every area of human understanding, with due regard to the differences in method appropriate to the various fields of knowledge and research. Our argument, however, suggests that in the search for a 'point of contact' between the divine and the human, reason does not hold a uniquely privileged place and that there are other dimensions of life which are equally (and, indeed, more urgently) relevant to spiritual development.

In his sermon on 'The Spiritual Presence' Paul Tillich spoke of some of the ways in which the presence of Spirit makes itself felt outside its, so to speak, public domain in the life of the Church:

> The Spirit can work in you with a soft but insistent voice, telling you that your life is empty and meaningless, but that there are chances of a new life waiting before the door of your inner self to fill its inner void and conquer its dulness. The Spirit can work in

you, awakening the desire to strive towards the sublime against the profanity of the average day. The Spirit can give you the courage that says 'yes' to life in spite of the destructiveness you have experienced around you and within you. The Spirit can reveal to you that you have hurt somebody deeply, but it can also give you the right word that reunites him with you. The Spirit can make you love, with the divine love, someone you profoundly dislike or in whom you have no interest. The Spirit can conquer your sloth towards what you know is the aim of your life, and it can transform your moods of aggression and depression into stability and serenity.[12]

These examples reveal manifestations of the spiritual life that are not primarily to do with our capacity for reason but have more to do with that whole world of feeling of relationships – what theologians of Tillich's generation called 'existential' – that constitutes such a large part of our life. But they also reflect situations and experiences that belong to human beings of all beliefs and none. They are not movements of the Spirit that are specifically available only to those within the Church nor to those (like artists) who might claim a special propensity for 'spirituality'. They are rather illustrations of the kind of spiritual revelation and the kind of spiritual testing that occurs continually in human life on earth – and the list could, of course, be extended almost indefinitely (especially if, with Teilhard, we believe that the presence of the Spirit pulses within the furthest reaches of matter). Without demanding conscious recognition such choices and challenges, such points of growth and transformation, are the stuff of life. They are what determines, in a very real and very basic sense, our character, who we are. They are that of which we are made and – recall the parable of the sheep and the goats – they shape us not merely as 'personalities' in the context of our everyday social dealings with one another but as who we are in the sight of eternity.

But, some might say, doesn't this, in effect, re-introduce a kind of predestination? If who we are is dependent on a kind of spiritual presence and a kind of spiritual activity that occurs at the levels of biology, of pre- and sub-conscious psychological life, of social interaction outside the scope of that rational understanding that alone makes free decision-making possible – then how can we be held responsible for who we are and for what we do? Aren't we back to the unacceptable face of Calvinism, only in a slightly modernised version, with biology and psychology replacing (or at least masking) the inscrutable and unfathomable pre-determining will of God? Far from the Spirit setting us free, this Spirit seems to be no more than a metaphor for our lack of freedom!

To answer this objection fully would require an extensive theological treatise. The issue is, after all, one which has troubled theology for many centuries and the name of 'Calvin' indicates only one of many points at which it has become urgent and controversial – one might find it, for example, in Paul, Augustine, Luther, Pascal. All we wish to say at present is therefore that in being open to such a charge we are in good company – and could it be otherwise? For doesn't any 'theology', that is, any attempt to understand human life by reference to God, mean that, at some point the modern ideal of a completely autonomous, completely self-determining, completely free human subject have to face the mystery that may be variously indicated by such words as 'creation' and 'grace'? In other words, that in relation to God 'It is he that hath made us and not we ourselves', so that the dangerous but beautiful mystery of personality, of the freedom that we are, is rooted and grounded in the still more dangerous and still more beautiful mystery of divine personality. This is the final frontier which can never be crossed but to which, in our exploring, in our reasoning, in our praying and in our self-sacrificial serving, we come again and again and where, each time we arrive, we must make the choice either to humble ourselves under grace or to condemn ourselves again to wander as strangers and pilgrims across that lonely wilderness lit by the proud but ambiguous star of individual and collective ego.

Spirit and Tradition (Again)

If, as we have argued, the life of the Spirit is present far beyond the narrow limits of the visible Church, in places and in ways where it is never acknowledged as such, what are the implications of such a vision for those who live within the discipline of the Church, whose faith is made actual by their participation in the process we have described as Spirit-and-Tradition? Is our tradition, is the life of the Church, in any way a privileged position with respect to the truth of spiritual existence – and, if not (to put it crudely), why bother? Why struggle to maintain the tradition – the historic, objective tradition of faith – against the world? (Or, to put the question in a less adversarial, more mission-oriented way) Why throw ourselves into the task of communicating that tradition to the world if the world is already a place within which the Spirit is at work?

With such questions we are again on territory that has been fought over many times in the course of the Church's history. They are, of course, remarkably similar to the questions raised by Paul in relation to Judaism, questions summed up in the question 'What advantage is there, then, in being a Jew ...?' (Romans 3.1). Even though he was able, in reply, to list a number of such 'advantages' he was clear that, in the light of the grace revealed in Christ, they could not be regarded as ultimate or finally decisive in any way. Jew and Gentile were ultimately equal before both the demand and the promise of God. We might think again of Barth's image of the dry canal and his warning that though the canal was channelled out by the living water of the Spirit nothing can compel the Spirit to continue to flow there. Is this, then, what we today, after two thousand years of Christianity, must say of the Church – that it plays the same ambiguous role as Judaism played for Paul in the Church's own formative years?

Certainly we would not wish to hide from the judgement implied in such a view. Isn't it rather a suspicious undertaking in any theology to try to define and stand on our own rights over against God? Can we really believe with a good conscience that our institutional adherence can constrain God's freedom? Do we really want to enter into unedifying calculations that are no more than spiritual haggling?

Let us take, as a very relevant example, the question of spiritual gifts. Clearly there has been a very strong strand in the Church's teaching and practice, a strand re-animated in recent times by the charismatic movement, that claims to identify certain spiritual gifts as the unique property of Christians, something we've got that others haven't, clear proof of who's in and who's out. This, then, is our 'advantage' – that we can speak in tongues, handle serpents, heal or experience that manifestation known as 'being slain by the Spirit'.

Interestingly, Paul deals with this question immediately following his rehearsal of the words of institution, a text we have used as a paradigm for the process of Spirit-and-Tradition. This in turn leads on to what is perhaps Paul's best-known chapter, the great eulogy on love of 1 Corinthians 13. Our reading, it may be recalled, understood Tradition out of the model of the Church's communication of itself to itself, the Church's self-creation, as that occurs 'in, with and under' the Eucharist, the memorial of the Lord's supper. This is not, as we stated and as the whole structure of this part of Paul's letter emphasizes, simply a matter of self-creation through the performance of ritual action. The ritualised act of remembrance, of re-call (in however full a sense that is understood), is rather a self-representation on the part of the community of what it is or is called to be. The 'truth' of the sacrament is interdependent with the character of the community that enacts it. The quality of the love, described definitively in chapter 13, in which the community meets is neither a more or less necessary preliminary to nor a result of the effective enactment of the sacrament. It is consubstantial with it. This is what Paul here understands as the supreme gift of the Spirit, 'the more excellent way'. The handing over of the body of Christ to the Church in the Eucharist is, in the context of such love, a real presence, a real manifestation of the Spirit and the Church itself is, in such an action, Spirit-filled.

Thinking through our question regarding the presence of Spirit 'inside' and 'outside' the Church in the light of this understanding of the Eucharistic presence of Spirit we may say this: that *in* the Church, as that which *differentiates* the Church, as the *advantage* of the Church, there is a *tradition of Spirit*. This does not in any way exclude any isolated or continuous manifestations of Spirit outside the Church. What it does is claim for the Church a very definite ordering of Spirit, namely, the ordering that is provided by its agapeistic memory of Christ, under the figure of His Supper – understanding 'memory' in Berdyaev's sense as an anticipation of the resurrection-world and not merely as the 'historical' memory of what happened long ago. Here Spirit is acknowledged and *communicated* (with the emphasis being on the 'communicated'), given a worldly shape, a continuing incarnation.

Does this make the 'difference' between the Church and the world merely one of knowledge: that here, in the Church, we know Spirit for what it is, we name it as the Spirit of God and as the Spirit of Christ – whereas in the world it remains, literally, anonymous? Again we must be wary of spiritual haggling and we must bear in mind the warning contained in the image of the dry canal. Yet simply identifying the 'difference' with such a shift in consciousness, a shift that doesn't necessarily involve any actual spiritual change or development, a shift in how we see things rather than in how we really are, doesn't seem to do justice to theology or (more importantly) experience.

But that is not all we are saying. What happens in the Church is not simply the finding of new and better names for old and familiar experiences (though it is remarkable how much 'proper' naming can transform our experience of the world!). What we have been proposing is a model based on communication, not on 'knowledge' or 'naming' but communication as communion, as a real process of transmitting, of handing over, in faith, of Christ-life, of Spirit-life – even if such communication is not always consciously 'at the front of our minds'. Such an 'advantage' is, as those who enjoy it will not hesitate to affirm, real enough – but what is there in it that implies a 'disadvantage' for those on the 'outside'? They (and, many Christians will readily admit, 'they' are 'we' for much of the time!) are not excluded from the life of the Spirit, which enters into and informs and is manifest in their experience and their action in innumerable ways.

Are we, then, saying that the relationship between 'inside' and 'outside' is like that between travellers at different stages on the same journey? That we on the 'inside' are simply further down the same road that the secular traveller or the traveller of another tradition is also treading? Or, if this image still seems to imply an unwarranted claim to superiority, is it perhaps a matter of different paths converging, more or less directly, on the same goal, the same promised land? Or, moving away from the language of pilgrimage and journey, we might ask whether the Church, then, is simply the opening of a special sacred space within the world, a clearing in the great forest of symbols out of which human beings build their world-pictures and self-images? There are risks with all such images – and it is perhaps a wise caution to remember that in such matters we usually do deal in metaphors and parables, in language which is not the language of exact science. All we seek is to affirm the reality of Spirit in the Church *and* the reality of Spirit outside the Church, to speak of 'advantage' within the Church, whilst not speaking of 'disadvantage' without! Given the limitations of language and metaphor, however, let us once again turn to Berdyaev for words in which to sum up what we have been striving to express. Berdyaev, it should be said, was as aware as anyone of the historical failures of the Church. Growing up in Russia prior to the revolution he lamented the historic Church's lack of prophetic concern for the victims of social injustice under the Czars and its apparent preoccupation with 'other-worldly' religious affairs. Yet, instead of shrinking his vision to fit the limitations of the Church as it appears in history, the Church as he encountered it, he projected a greater vision, a vision that recalled the language of Ephesians and Colossians as of the Orthodox liturgy itself.

> The life of the Church rests upon holy tradition and succession. It is through tradition that in each new generation man enters into the same spiritual world. Tradition is ... the creative spiritual life transmitted from generation to generation, uniting the living and the dead and thereby overcoming death. Death reigns in the world indeed but it is vanquished in the Church. Tradition is the memory which brings resurrection, the victory over corruption, the affirmation of eternal life ... [In this sense] ... The Church is not a reality existing side by side with others; it is not an element in the historic and universal whole; it is not a separated objective reality. The Church is all; it constitues the

whole plenitude of being, of the life of humanity, and of the world in a state of Christianization ... It is in the Church that the grass grows and the flowers blossom, for the Church is nothing less than the cosmos Christianized. Christ enters the cosmos, He was crucified and rose again within it, and thereby all things were made new, the whole cosmos follows his footsteps to crucifixion and to resurrection.

And, he continues,

Beauty is the Christianized cosmos in which chaos is overcome; that is why the Church may be defined as the true beauty of existence. Every achievement of beauty in the world is in the deepeset sense a process of Christianization. Beauty is the goal of all life; it is the deification of the world.[13]

If 'deification' (literally: 'being made into God') sounds like a return to pagan ideas of deifying nature, it should be said that the Eastern tradition of Christianity regularly uses such bold language to describe the ultimate goal of the Christian life, thereby drawing out and emphasizing the full magnitude of what is implied in Paul's words in 2 Corinthians 3.13–18:

... where the Spirit of the Lord is, there is freedom. And we, who with unveiled faces all reflect the Lord's glory, are being transformed into his likeness with ever-increasing glory, which comes from the Lord, who is the Spirit.

As we look – both inwards and outwards – at the situation of the Church on the threshold of a new millennium we ask: Will any lesser vision do?

Notes

Chapter 1

1. David Lodge, *How Far Can You Go?* (Harmondsworth: Penguin, 1981) p. 89.
2. Mark Schaaf, 'Dutch Catholic Theology'. *Cross Currents*. Winter, 1973. No. 4, p. 426.
3. Decree 'Lamentabili' and encyclical 'Pascendi'. Also the modernist oath, required of all priests on ordination, until relatively recent times.
4. Thomas Hardy, *Collected Poems*. (London, Macmillan, 1976) p. 561.
5. W. O. Chadwick *From Bossuet to Newman* (Cambridge, C.U.P., 1957)
6. Op. cit. p. 19.
7. p. 66.
8. Op. cit. p. 100 and *Essay*. Introduction, p. 43.
9. J. H. Newman, p. 185. *An Essay on the Development of Christian Doctrine* (Pelican Edition Harmondsworth, 1974.)
10. Op. cit. pp. 270–272.
11. pp. 70–71.
12. p. 100.
13. University Sermon, 2 February 1843.
14. *Essay*, p. 352.
15. University Sermon, 2 February 1843.
16. *Essay*, p. 352.
17. *Essay*, p. 364.
18. Chadwick, p. 102.
19. Op. cit. p. 147.

Chapter 2

1. *The Nature of Christian Belief*. The House of Bishops of the Church of England. (London, Church House Publishing, 1986.)
2. 'Can Doctrine Develop?' *The Times*, Monday 2nd June, 1986.
3. Op. cit. Final paragraph. (The Bishop of London at that time was The Rt Revd Dr Graham Leonard who has since his retirement become a Roman Catholic.)
4. J. H. Newman, *An Essay on the Development of Christian Doctrine*. (Harmondsworth: Penguin, 1974), p. 163. He goes on also to use the parables of the seed growing secretly and of the leaven, pp. 163, 153.
5. So John Thurmer, *A Detection of the Trinity*. (Exeter, Paternoster Press, 1984) Cf. p. 11 and p. 41. 'One might deduce the Trinitarian nature of God from the *Old* Testament, but one could not deduce the Christian terminology.'
6. J. D. G. Dunn. *Christology in the Making*. (London: SCM Press, 1980). C. F. D. Moule. *The Origins of Christology*. (Cambridge, C.U.P. 1977, etc.)
7. Thomas Torrance, *The Trinitarian Faith*, (Edinburgh, T&T Clark, 1988) p. 24.
8. James Mackey, *The Christian Experience of God as Trinity* (London, SCM Press, 1983) p. 2.
9. Op. cit. pp. 124–130, 164–167.
10. Cf. Maurice Wiles, *Working Papers in Doctrine*. (London: SCM Press, 1976) p. 21.
11. Sarah Coakley, 'Can God be Experienced as Trinity?' *Modern Churchman*, XXXVIII, No. 2, 1986, p. 14, quoting also Andrew Louth, *The Origins of the Christian Mystical Tradition*. (Oxford: O.U.P., 1981) pp. 75 f.

12. Coakley, op. cit. p. 14. She suggests that Mackey can see no account that can preserve the orthodox holding together of three hypostases in the one substance.

13. This is one of the main points of criticism that may be placed against the revised rites of initiation in the Church of England, where the activity of the three persons of the divine Trinity are differentiated very sharply under creation redemption, and sanctification.

14. E.g. cause, being directly caused, and being indirectly caused.

15. Cf. Maurice Wiles, *The Making of Christian Doctrine*. (Cambridge: C.U.P., 1967) pp. 135–136.

16. Maurice Wiles, *Working Papers in Doctrine*. (SCM Press.) op. cit. p. 1 f'Some Reflections on the Origins of the Doctrine of the Trinity'. J. L. Houlden, *Exploration in Theology*. (SCM Press. 3. London, 1978.) Pp. 25. ff.

17. G. W. H. Lampe, *God as Spirit*, (Oxford: O.U.P, 1977)

18. Mackey, ad 1 oc.

19. Lampe, op. cit., p. 144.

20. Mackey, op. cit., for example p. 230.

21. David Brown, *The Divine Trinity*. (London, Duckworth, 1985).

22. Brown, Ibid, p. 4. See also p. 236.

23. Coakley, op. cit. pp. 20 ff.

24. Cf. Mackey, op. cit. Cf. also most of the recent writings of Don Cupitt and also the implications of his television documentaries for Christianity.

25. Coakley, op. cit., p. 21.

26. *We Believe in God*, Church of England Doctrine Commission, (London. Church House Publishing, 1987). Ch. 7, p. 111.

27. Robin Lane-Fox, *Pagans and Christians* (London: Viking, 1986), especially chapters 1–5.

28. Vincent J. Donovan, *Christianity Rediscovered: An Epistle from the Masai*. (London, SCM Press, 1982) p. 163.

Chapter 3

1. Karl Barth, *The Epistle to the Romans* (Oxford: Oxford University Press, 1933) pp. 65–6.

2. See *Heritage and Prophecy – Grundtvig and the English-Speaking Word*, Edited by A. M. Allchin, D. Jasper, J. H. Schørring and K. Stevenson (The Canterbury Press Norwich, 1994).

3. Quoted in E. L. Allen, *Bishop Grundtvig: A Prophet of the North* (London: James Clarke) p. 65.

4. Allen, p. 75.

5. *Den Danske Salme Bog*, 1953, Numbers 250, 253 and 283.

6. Quoted in J. T. Burtchael, *Catholic Theories of Biblical Inspiration Since 1810* (Cambridge: Cambridge University Press, 1969) p. 18.

7. Yves Congar, *Tradition and Traditions* (London: Burns and Oates, 1966) pp. 268–9.

8. Ibid., pp. 264–5.

9. Ibid., p. 263.

10. Nicholas Berdyaev, *Freedom and the Spirit* (London: Geoffrey Bles, 1935) pp. 330–1.

11. Nicholas Berdyaev, *Slavery and Freedom* (London: Geoffrey Bles, 1943) p. 111.

Chapter 4

1. In H. W. Bartsch (ed.), *Kerygma and Myth A Theological Debate* (London: SPCK, 1972), p. 5.

2. Adolf Harnack, *What is Christianity?* (London: 1901), p. 125.

3. Ibid., p. 129.

4. R. Bultmann, *History and Eschatology* (Edinburgh: Edinburgh University Press, 1975) p. 11.

5. In R. Bultmann, *Existence and Faith* (London: Fontana, 1964) pp. 342–52.

6. C. H. Dodd, *The Parables of the Kingdom* (London: Nisbet, 1935), pp. 11f.

7. All quotations are taken from Avril Henry (ed.) *Biblia Pauperum* (New York: Cornell University Press, 1987).

8. Northrop Frye, *The Great Code: The Bible and Literature* (London: Routledge and Kegan Paul, 1982), p. 81.

9. Ibid., p. 25.

10. From the German edition: E. Cardenal, *Das Evangelium der Bauern von Solentiname* (Wuppertal, 1976), p. 11.

Chapter 5

1. *The Anglican/Roman Catholic International Commission I & II, Final Report* (London, CTS/SPCK, 1982). *The Malta Report* (London 1968) included in the Final Report publication.

2. *Vatican Response to the Arcic I* (December 1991, CTS, London). Women in the Priesthood Declaration. *Inter insigniores.* (Rome, 1976).

3. cf. Robert L. Wilken. *The Myth of Christian Beginnings.* (London, SCM Press, 1979.)

4. Vincent Donovan. *Christianity Rediscovered.* Ad loc.

5. Wilken, op cit p. 104 ff.

6. Stephen Sykes, *The Identity of Christianity*, (London, SPCK, 1984) p. 284.

Chapter 6

1. Austin Farrer, *Finite and Infinite.* (London, Dacre Press, 1943) p. 299.

2. Austin Farrer, *A Celebration of Faith.* Edited J. L. Houlden. (London. Hodder and Stoughton 1970) p. 15.

3. Austin Farrer, *A Rebirth of Images.* (London Dacre Press. 1949). Austin Farrer, *The Revelation of St John the Divine: a Commentary.* (Oxford, O.U.P., 1964).

4. Austin Farrer, *Love Almighty and Ills Unlimited.* (London, Fontana Press, 1962).

5. Austin Farrer, *A Rebirth of Images.* op. cit. p. 13.

6. See his contribution to *Kerygma and Myth.* Edited H. W. Bartsch. (London, SPCK, 1953.) p. 222 ff.

7. Charles Williams, *The Image of the City.* (Oxford, O.U.P.) p. 147 ff.

8. Austin Farrer, *The Crown of the Year.* (London, Dacre Press, 1952) p. 47.

9. Austin Farrer, *The Brink of Mystery.* (London, SPCK, 1976) p. 126 ff.

10. Austin Farrer. *The Glass of Vision.* (London, Dacre Press, 1948) p. 8.

11. *The Glass of Vision*, op cit. p. 28.

12. op. cit. p. 29.

13. op. cit. p. 59.

14. op. cit. p. 74.

15. op. cit. p. 89.

16. op. cit. p. 129.

17. R. E. C. Browne, *The Ministry of the Word.* (London, SCM Press) pp. 86–87.

18. Charles Williams, *The Place of the Lion* (Grand Rapids: Eerdmans, 1991) pp. 14–15. Further references are indicated in the main text as PL.

19. In C. G. Jung et al., *Man and His Symbols* (London: Aldus Books, 1964), p. 159.

20. Ibid., p. 174.

Chapter 7

1. In L. Ouspensky and V. Lossky, *The Meaning of Icons* (New York: St. Vladimir's Seminary Press, 1983) p. 15.

2. In *The Journey. A Search for the Role of Contemporary Art in Religious and Spiritual Life* (Lincoln: Usher Gallery with Redcliffe Press, 190), p. 83.

3. Jacques Maritain, *Art and Scholasticism* (London: Sheed and Ward, 1933), p. 52.
4. Umberto Eco, *Art and Beauty in the Middle Ages* (Newhaven: Yale University Press, 1986), p. 76.
5. Peter Fuller, 'Crisis of Faith in Modern Art' in *The Sunday Telegraph* 17.6 1990, Review p. 11.
6. Don Cupitt, 'The Abstract Sacred' in *The Journey* (op. cit.), p. 103.
7. A. Pugin, *Contrasts* (London, 1841), p. 3.
8. *Contrasts*, p. 4.
9. A. Pugin, *An Apology for the Revival of Christian Architecture in England* (London, 1843), p. 7.
10. Both references are to John Ruskin, *The Seven Lamps of Architecture* (London: Cassell, 1919) p. 155.
11. Eric Gill, *The Necessity of Belief* (London: Faber and Faber, 1936), p. 337.
12. John Henry Newman, *On the Scope and Nature of University Education* (London: Everyman, 1915), p. 64.
13. Quinlan Terry, 'Origins of the Orders' in *Architectural Review*, Vol. 173, no. 1032, Feb. 1983., p. 33. Hereafter *AR*.
14. Idem., 'Genuine Classicism' in *RIBA Transactions 3* (Vol. 2, no. 1), 1983, pp. 6f. Hereafter *RIBA*.
15. Quoted in Tim Barton, 'The Sacred and the Search for Myths' in *Le Corbusier: Architect of the Century*. (London: Arts Council, 1987), p. 238.
16. *Architect of the Century*, p. 240.
17. *Architect of the Century*, p. 246.
18. Tim Gough, 'Corpus Christi, Aachen' in *Church Building*, p. 23.
19. John Tinsley, 'Romanesque Religion' in *Tell it Slant*. (Bristol, Indiana: Wyndham Hall Press, 1990), p. 105.
20. Allan Doig, 'Taking Risks' in *Church Building*, Issue 15, Summer 1990, p. 2.
21. H. Rombach, *Leben des Geistes*, (Freiburg-im-Breisgau: Herder, 1977) p. 8 (my translation).
22. *Contrasts*, p. 47.
23. A. Trollope, *The Warden* (London: Everyman Edn, 1907), p. 240.

Chapter 8

1. Quoted in Henry Bettenson (ed.), *Documents of the Christian Church* (London: Oxford University Press, 1943), p. 6.
2. Augustine, *Confessions* VII:9 (Harmondsowrth: Penguin, 1961), p. 146.
3. *Confessions* VII:21, p. 156.
4. Richard Hooker, *Ecclesiastical Polity*. Vol. 1 (London and New York: Dent Dutton Everyman edn., 1907) pp. 176f.
5. In E. Brunner and Karl Barth, *Natural Theology*. (London: Geoffrey Bles, 1946) p. 74.
6. *Works of Ralph Waldo Emerson* (London: Routledge) pp. 560–1.
7. Pierre Teilhard de Chardin, *The Phenomenon of Man* (London: Collins Fontana, 1965) pp. 69–70.
8. Pierre Teilhard de Chardin, *Hymn of the Universe* (London: Collins Fontana, 1970) p. 60, pp. 64f.
9. John V. Taylor, *The Go-Between God* (London: SCM Press, 1972), p. 31.
10. C. G. Jung *Memories, Dreams and Reflections* (London: Collins Fontana, 1967) pp. 172–3.
11. C. G. Jung, *Modern Man in Search of a Soul* (London: Routledge and Kegan Paul, 1933), p. 253.
12. Paul Tillich, *The Boundaries of Our Being* (London: Collins Fontana, 1973) pp. 70–1.
13. Nicholas Berdyaev, *Freedom and the Spirit* (London: Geoffrey Bles, 1935) pp. 330–2.